The YOUTH SOCCER Handbook

Learn the Fundamentals, Sharpen Your Skills,
and Develop Winning Strategies
to Dominate the Pitch

Pathways Press

TABLE OF CONTENTS

Introduction.. 1

Chapter 1: The Basics 5

The Origin of Soccer... 6

Modern Game Development 7

A Sport Without Borders...................................... 8

A New Generation of Stars................................... 9

Benefits of Playing Soccer 10

It's Great for Your Body 10

It Boosts Your Mental Skills 11

It Teaches Teamwork 11

It Makes You More Confident 11

You Make Friends 11

It Relieves Stress 12

It Improves Your Discipline and Focus 12

It's Accessible to Everyone 12

It Opens Doors to New Opportunities 13

It's Just Plain Fun! 13

Overview of Soccer Positions and Their Roles........... 13

Goalkeeper (GK) 14

Key Responsibilities 15

Defenders 17

Midfielders 19

Forwards 22

Understanding the Game Flow 23

Basic Soccer Rules and Regulations 24

Game Structure 24

Scoring 24

Referees and Officials 24

Common Fouls and Offenses 25

Restarts and Set Pieces 25

Player Positions and Roles 26

Chapter 2: Essential Skills and Techniques 27

Passing and Receiving Techniques 28

Basic Pass Types 28

Receiving the Ball 30

Proper Body Positioning 30

Soft Touches for Control 30

Read the Ball's Trajectory! 30

Triangle Passing Drill 31

Long Ball Switch Drill 31

Through Ball Drill 32

Communication in Passing 32

Verbal Communication 32

Non-Verbal Cues 32

Dribbling Fundamentals 33

Basic Dribbling Techniques............................ 33

Footwork and Ball Control 35

Low Body Posture and Balance..................... 35

Situations 37

Avoiding Defenders 38

Shooting Accuracy and Power 40

The Mechanics Behind the Perfect Shot.................. 41

Where to Aim and Why It Matters 43

Shooting Drills.. 44

Basic Defending Skills 47

Fundamentals of Positioning........................ 47

Tackling Techniques.................................... 49

Marking the Opponent................................. 50

Building a Defensive Unit............................. 52

Chapter 3: Advanced Skill Development...................... 55

Body Trapping Techniques 56

Feet 56

Thighs.. 57

Chest.. 57

Footwork Drills for Control 57

Cone Dribbling With Traps.......................... 58

First Touch Circuits 58

Wall Pass Control....................................... 58

Using Space and Time 59

Anticipating Ball Trajectories 59

Positioning Your Body in Space..................... 59

Overcoming Pressure 59

Advanced Dribbling Moves.. 61

    Feints and Fakes.. 61

Change of Pace and Direction..................................... 62

Using Both Feet 63

    Creating Space With Dribbling............................... 64

Precision Shooting Under Pressure 65

    Shooting Drills With Variations............................... 65

    The Mental Edge in Shooting................................. 67

    Finishing Techniques... 68

    Reacting to Defenders 69

Tackling and Interception Strategies............................ 70

    Types of Tackles... 71

    Interception Techniques... 72

    Defensive Positioning.. 73

    Team Defensive Strategies....................................... 75

Chapter 4: Team Strategies and Formations 77

    4-4-2 Formation 78

    4-3-3 Formation 78

    3-5-2 Formation 80

    5-3-2 Formation 80

    Roles and Responsibilities....................................... 80

    Verbal Communication 81

    Non-Verbal Communication.................................... 82

    Creating a Positive Communication Environment..... 83

    Analyzing Opponent Strengths and Weaknesses 83

    Flexible Formation Adjustments.............................. 83

    Responding to Game Progression 84

Learning From Matches 84

Chapter 5: The Mental Game 85

Developing Concentration and Focus 86

The Importance of Focus 87

Techniques to Improve Focus 87

Creating a Focus-Friendly Environment..................... 88

Tracking Progress 89

Overcoming Performance Anxiety:

Play Like the Pros Even Under Pressure 90

Understanding Anxiety's Impact.............................. 91

Coping Strategies for Anxiety................................. 91

Visualizing Success 92

Seeking Support 93

Goal Setting and Motivation 94

Visualization Techniques..................................... 96

Chapter 6: Fitness and Conditioning 99

Endurance Training for Soccer Players 99

Strength and Conditioning Exercises........................... 101

Flexibility and Injury Prevention:

Stay Agile, Stay Healthy 104

Soccer-Specific Agility Drills 107

Chapter 7: Nutrition for Peak Performance............. 109

Balanced Diet Essentials for Young Athletes.................. 110

Macronutrients 111

Micronutrients: The Little Things

That Make a Big Difference 112

Meal Timing: Eating Like a Pro 112

Healthy Snack Options: Power up on the Go 113

Hydration and Its Importance:

Fuel Your Game With Water 114

Pre-Game and Post-Game Nutrition Tips:

Fuel Up, Recover Strong 117

Timing Your Meals: When to Eat 118

Post-Game Recovery: Rebuild and Recharge 119

Tracking Your Nutrition: Find What Works Best for

You 120

Key Takeaway 120

Supplements: Pros and Cons—What You Need to

Know 120

Key Takeaway 124

Chapter 8: Off-Season Training 125

Off-Season Training Routines 126

Creating a Balanced Training Schedule 126

Incorporating Individual Skill Drills 126

Simulating Game Scenarios 127

Monitoring Progress and Adaptations 127

Key Takeaways 128

Importance of Rest and Recovery 128

Cross-Training Benefits 131

Key Takeaways 133

Setting Personal Goals for Off-Season Training 133

Creating SMART Goals 133

Reflection on Past Performance 134

Breaking Larger Goals Into Milestones 135

Accountability and Support Systems 135

Key Takeaways 135

Chapter 9: Building Team Chemistry 137

Importance of Trust and Respect 138

Building Trust Through Communication 138

Respecting Each Player's Role 139

Handling Conflicts With Respect 139

Creating a Safe Space for Vulnerability 140

Key Takeaways: 140

Team-Building Activities and Exercises 141

The goal of the Subpoint 141

Set of Supporting Ideas 141

Key Takeaways 142

Encouraging Open Communication............................. 142

Goal of the Subpoint.. 142

Set of Supporting Ideas 143

Key Takeaways 144

Role of Leadership Within the Team 144

Key Takeaways 146

Chapter 10: Game Day Preparation 147

Pre-Match Rituals and Routines 147

Key Takeaways 149

Pre-Match Rituals and Routines:

The Power of Warm-Up Exercises and Stretches.... 150

Key Takeaways 152

Pre-Match Rituals and Routines:

Scouting the Opponent 152

Research and Observation 153

Team Collaboration 153

Adjusting Mindset 154

Practice Scenarios.. 154

Key Takeaways 155

Structured Reflection.. 155

Team Feedback.. 156

Mental Reinforcement.. 156

Setting Future Goals... 157

Conclusion 159

References.. 163

INTRODUCTION

Have you ever felt the thrilling rush of scoring a goal in front of a cheering crowd, knowing that every ounce of hard work in training has led to this moment? Welcome to The Youth Soccer Handbook, your ultimate guide to becoming a better soccer player and teammate. Whether you're a seasoned player looking to sharpen your skills or a newcomer eager to learn, this handbook is designed just for you.

Soccer is more than just a game; it's an adventure full of teamwork, strategy, and personal growth. Imagine the excitement of running onto the pitch with your teammates, each of you ready to give your best. This book will help you make the most of these moments and provide you with everything you need to excel. From nailing down fundamental techniques to understanding complex strategies, we've got you covered. But more than that, it will teach you how to be a valuable team member and cultivate a love for the sport that goes beyond the field.

Why play soccer? It's not just about physical fitness, although chasing the ball up and down the field will keep you in shape. It's also about developing key life skills like discipline, communication, and teamwork. These qualities will serve you well on and off the pitch. When you play soccer, you're building muscle and stamina— and you're building character. You're learning how to work with others toward a common goal, share victories, and handle defeats gracefully.

Many young players want to jump straight into advanced moves and flashy skills, but without a solid foundation, you'll struggle to improve. Think of it like building a house: if the foundation isn't strong, the whole structure is shaky. By focusing on the fundamentals, you'll set yourself up for long-term success. This is where this book will help you.

This handbook is laid out in a way that's easy to follow to ensure you get the most out of every chapter. Each section is packed with practical advice and exercises to integrate into your training sessions. Whether you want to improve your dribbling, become a master passer, or understand the intricacies of different game formations, each chapter builds on the previous one to ensure comprehensive development.

Besides physical skills, soccer is also a mental game. Being mentally tough means staying focused, managing stress, and keeping a positive attitude—even when things don't go your way. In tough matches, the mentally strong players often outperform equally skilled but less resilient opponents. This book will introduce you to techniques such as visualization and goal-setting, which are essential tools for any serious athlete. These mental strategies don't just help on the field—they're useful skills for school and other aspects of your life.

Soccer is a team sport, and understanding how to communicate effectively with all the other skills you'll learn here can make all the difference. Good communication ensures everyone knows their role and can anticipate each other's movements. It helps you celebrate victories as a group and navigate losses constructively. We'll dive deep into how you can enhance your teamwork skills, making you a player everyone wants on their side.

The off-season is a golden opportunity to continue improving without the pressure of games. We'll provide you with routines to keep your skills sharp and your body in peak condition. This way, when the new season starts, you'll hit the ground running—literally.

Nutrition plays a huge role in how you perform, from giving you the energy to run those sprints to helping your muscles recover after a tough match. We'll cover what you must eat and drink before and after games to keep your body fueled and hydrated. Knowing how to feed your body properly is like having a secret weapon—it gives you that extra edge over your competition.

Finally, game day preparation is key to performing well. A pre-match routine can help settle those nerves and get you into the right mindset. From warming up correctly to mentally visualizing how you want to play, there are numerous little rituals that can set you up for success. And once the game is over, analyzing your performance helps identify what went well and what could be improved. This continuous learning cycle turns every match into a stepping stone toward becoming a better player.

So gear up because this journey through The Youth Soccer Handbook is bound to be exciting and rewarding. With every page, you'll gather tools and tips to help you dominate the pitch. Remember, soccer isn't just about the final score—it's about enjoying the game, building friendships, and growing both as a player and an individual. Ready to step up your game? Let's get started!

CHAPTER 1:
THE BASICS

Way before Messi and Ronaldo, ancient civilizations like China, Greece, and Rome played early versions of the game. Even medieval Europe had its chaotic ball games that influenced the sport we love today! Each of these cultures added their flair, which set the foundation for modern soccer.

In this introductory chapter, we'll dive into the key moments that transformed soccer into the global phenomenon it is today—starting with 19th-century England, where the game became more organized with standardized rules. You'll see how this change helped turn a chaotic pastime into the thrilling, skillful game we know and can't get enough of.

In the second part of the chapter, we'll break down the basics of soccer—covering the positions on the field, the roles each player has, and the standard rules that make the game tick. By the end, you'll understand why soccer has remained the world's favorite sport for so long and why it is more than just fun—it's a chance to be part of a game that has connected people across centuries!

THE ORIGIN OF SOCCER

The beginnings of soccer aren't as clean-cut as the modern game we know today, with its perfect pitches and precise rules. Back then, soccer's early forms were wild and untamed, a beautiful chaos that reflected the passion of its players.

One of the earliest examples comes from China's Han Dynasty (206 BCE – 220 CE), where soldiers played a game called Cuju. In this game, players kicked a leather ball filled with feathers into a small net. Cuju spread from military training exercises to a popular sport across the empire.

Meanwhile, in ancient Greece and Rome, similar ball games existed, though they were often rougher and more physical. These games, like Episkyros in Greece and Harpastum in Rome, were played in teams and involved a ball, but the rules were loosely defined. There was no standard field, no formal teams, and, quite frankly, not much concern for safety. These ancient games reveal a simple truth: people have always loved to kick things for fun!

As centuries passed, medieval Europe saw its versions of soccer, often called "mob football". In English villages, entire towns would participate in wild matches where almost anything went—hundreds of players would try to kick an inflated animal bladder toward a distant goal. The creativity of these early players helped shape the rules and structure that modern soccer would later adopt.

Modern Game Development

Soccer didn't truly become "soccer" until the mid-19th century in England. By then, schools and clubs began to see the need for a standardized set of rules. 1863, the Football Association was founded in England, and the first official set of rules—known as the Laws of the Game—was established.

These laws formed the foundation of modern soccer, focusing on fairness, sportsmanship, and structure. Gone were the days of "mob football" madness, replaced by 11 players on each side, a clear field, and an organized approach to scoring goals.

As soccer began to spread, countries worldwide embraced the game, each adding its flavor to it. The Federation International de Football Association (FIFA) was founded in 1904, bringing the global soccer community together under one organization.

FIFA helped formalize international competitions, including the birth of the World Cup in 1930, the first global tournament that crowned the best team in the world. Key changes to the rules throughout the 20th century helped soccer adapt to a modern audience.

A Sport Without Borders

What makes soccer so special is its ability to transcend borders. No matter where you are in the world, people play soccer. From dusty fields in Africa to high-tech stadiums in Europe, soccer brings people together. It's a language spoken by feet and hearts, making it one of the most inclusive sports ever.

Soccer has played a huge role in cultural exchange and unity. For instance, during times of war or political conflict, soccer often brought people together unexpectedly. One famous example is the "Christmas Truce" of 1914, during World War 1, when British and German soldiers temporarily stopped fighting to play soccer together in no man's land.

Soccer also has a long history of inspiring social change. For example, it became a tool for breaking racial barriers. The Brazilian legend Pelé, a Black man from a poor background, became a global superstar in the 1950s and 60s, proving that talent, not skin color, was what mattered most on the pitch. In recent decades, female soccer stars like Marta have used their platforms to fight for gender equality in sports, showing how soccer continues to influence cultural and social progress.

A New Generation of Stars

Soccer isn't just for pros on TV. Youth soccer has exploded around the world, giving kids the chance to follow in the footsteps of their heroes. In many countries, grassroots movements and local leagues create new opportunities for young players to shine. From school soccer teams to community leagues, kids are being nurtured as the next generation of talent.

These youth programs do more than just teach kids how to dribble or pass. They promote values like teamwork, discipline, and perseverance. Whether you're playing in a small-town league or a national youth academy, soccer teaches life lessons that go beyond the game.

In many countries, especially in the U.S., youth soccer has become a powerful tool for building healthy communities. It allows kids to stay active, form friendships, and dream big. Through these programs, kids learn that with dedication and hard work, they can achieve great things on the field—and in life.

Soccer is more than just a game—it's a global tradition, a symbol of unity, and a way of life for millions. Understanding its history and evolution helps young players appreciate their role in carrying the torch forward while recognizing the game's power to bring people together across time and space.

BENEFITS OF PLAYING SOCCER

Soccer gives you more than just a sweaty jersey and a few high-fives. It teaches teamwork, keeps you in killer shape, and boosts your confidence like nothing else. If you haven't laced up those cleats yet, you're missing out on a pretty epic journey.

It's Great for Your Body

Think about all the running, kicking, and quick turns in a soccer game. Every time you sprint down the field chasing the ball, you build up serious stamina, improving your endurance without even noticing. When you blast a shot at a goal or boot a long pass, you strengthen your leg muscles and core.

And those sudden pivots to dodge defenders? They're improving your agility and flexibility, making you quicker on your feet and more balanced. Whether defending, attacking, or just hustling back to cover, soccer is a full-body workout that keeps you in top shape!

It Boosts Your Mental Skills

Soccer is a game of strategy where you need to think fast, plan your moves, and communicate with your teammates. These skills help you improve problem-solving and decision-making, whether on the field or off. You'll learn how to read the game, anticipate what's coming next, and make quick choices while working as a team.

It Teaches Teamwork

Speaking of teams, soccer is the ultimate team sport. You can't win a game alone, which makes it so awesome! You'll learn to trust and rely on others, communicate clearly, and support your teammates, even when things get tough. Plus, that feeling of celebrating a goal together? It's one of the best in the world.

It Makes You More Confident

Scoring a goal, defending like a pro, or just improving your skills over time helps build your self-confidence. As you get better at the game, you'll notice yourself feeling more confident in other areas of life, too. It shows you that with practice and determination, you can achieve great things.

You Make Friends

Soccer is a great way to make new friends. Whether you join a school team or a local club or just play with friends at the park, soccer brings people together. It doesn't matter where you come from—soccer is a universal language that connects people worldwide. And the more you play, the more fun you'll have meeting people who share your passion.

It Relieves Stress

When life gets a bit overwhelming, soccer can be your escape. Running around, focusing on the game, and being outside in the fresh air are great ways to blow off steam. It helps you forget about stress, exams, or any other worries. Plus, exercise releases endorphins, the "feel-good" chemicals in your brain, so you'll always leave the field feeling better than when you started.

It Improves Your Discipline and Focus

In soccer, you must stick to a schedule, follow rules, and practice regularly if you want to improve. This helps build your discipline and teaches you the value of hard work and commitment. The focus you develop while playing soccer can also carry over into schoolwork and other activities.

It's Accessible to Everyone

Unlike some sports, soccer doesn't require tons of expensive gear. All you need is a ball and some space to play. Some of the greatest players, like Pelé and Marta, started their soccer journeys with nothing more than a makeshift ball—sometimes even a bundle of rags or a grapefruit—and a dirt patch to play on. They didn't have fancy cleats or high-end equipment, just passion and creativity. It shows that what matters in soccer isn't the gear but the drive to play, learn, and improve.

It Opens Doors to New Opportunities

If you're passionate about soccer and work hard at it, you could even end up with amazing opportunities. Scholarships, travel teams, or maybe even a future in professional soccer—it's all possible! And even if you don't go pro, the skills and friendships you develop through soccer will last a lifetime.

It's Just Plain Fun!

At the end of the day, soccer is fun! Whether you're playing competitively or just kicking the ball around with friends, the joy of the game is undeniable. The excitement of chasing the ball, the thrill of scoring, and the camaraderie with teammates make soccer an experience that's hard to beat.

OVERVIEW OF SOCCER POSITIONS AND THEIR ROLES

Soccer can seem complex to the average beginner with its multiple roles and regulations, but breaking it down into manageable parts makes it much easier to comprehend. Whether you're new to the game or looking to refine your knowledge, knowing who does what on the field and how the game flows will enhance your appreciation and involvement.

At its core, soccer is played by two teams, each typically consisting of 11 players, including a goalkeeper. Each position has unique responsibilities, which contribute to both offensive and defensive strategies. Here's a closer look at the main positions on the field and their roles:

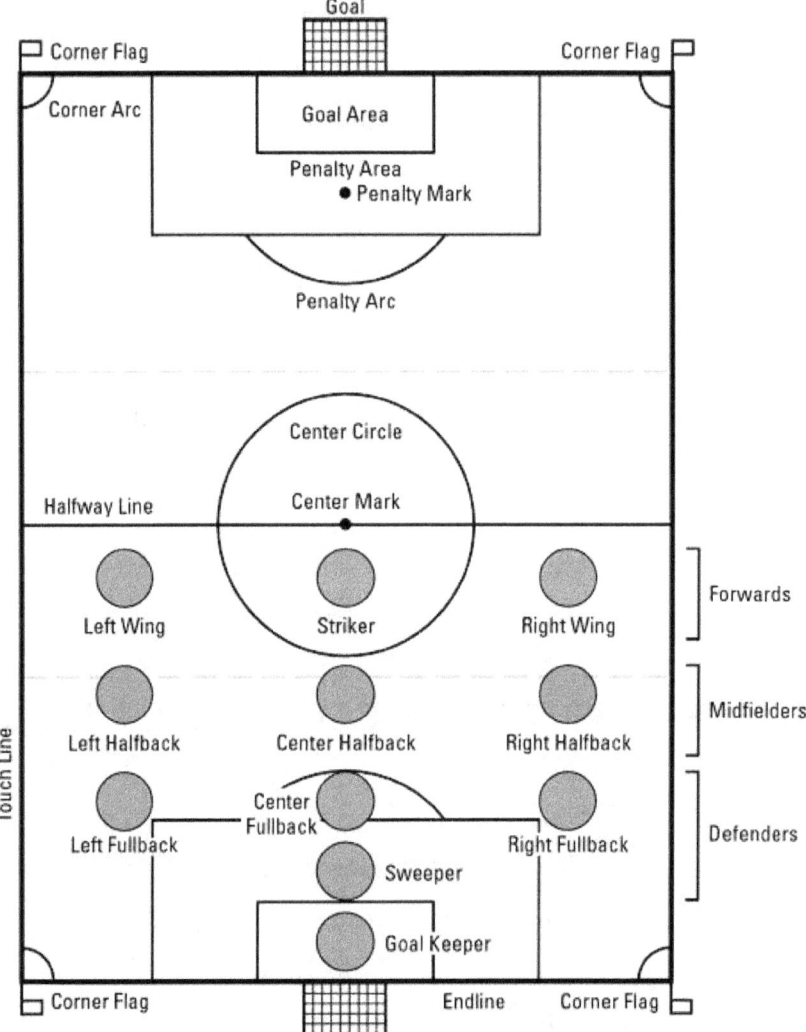

Goalkeeper (GK)

The goalkeeper is the last line of defense for your team, and they play a huge part in how successful the squad is. While it may look like all they do is guard the net, their role is much more complicated and requires a mix of unique skills. Let's break down what makes goalkeepers so important.

Key Responsibilities

Shot-Stopping

The most important job of a goalkeeper is to stop the other team from scoring. Here's what they need to do:

- **Diving:** Goalkeepers have to dive in different directions to block shots. They practice diving to stay safe and reach the ball as best as possible.
- **Positioning:** A good goalkeeper knows how to stand in the goal to cover as much area as possible. This means reading the game and predicting where the shots will come from.
- **Handling:** It's not just about stopping the ball; they also need to grab it securely so that attackers can't get another chance to score. They work on catching and controlling the ball to avoid dangerous rebounds.

Distribution

Once they make a save, the goalkeeper's work isn't done! How they get the ball back into play can change the game:

- **Kicking:** After a save, they can kick the ball far to start an attack with a goal kick or a quick pass to a teammate. A good kick can switch the game from defense to offense quickly.
- **Throwing:** Goalkeepers can also throw the ball to teammates to keep the play moving fast. A well-timed throw can surprise the other team and create opportunities.

- **Smart decisions:** Knowing when to pass quickly and when to hold onto the ball is key for controlling how the game flows.

Organizing Defense

Goalkeepers are like coaches on the field, helping to keep the team organized:

- **Communication:** They constantly talk to their defenders, giving instructions on where to stand and who to mark. This is especially important during set pieces, like corners or free kicks.
- **Reading the game:** Good goalkeepers can predict what the opposing team will do and give their teammates a heads-up about potential threats, helping everyone adjust their positions.
- **Initiating defensive shape:** By organizing the defense, goalkeepers ensure the team stays solid and knows their roles, especially when under pressure.

Essential Attributes

A good goalkeeper stays calm and confident, even after letting in a goal. This mental strength helps them bounce back and focus on the rest of the game. They also need quick reflexes to react fast, strong core muscles to dive effectively, and good hand-eye coordination to make saves. On top of that, they must understand the game well to anticipate plays and keep track of their defenders, adjusting their position based on what's happening on the field.

Good Examples

- **Manuel Neuer:** Known as one of the best goalkeepers ever, Neuer is famous for his quick reflexes and smart positioning. If you've seen any of his matches, you'll know how his quick reflexes and smart positioning allow him to stop shots that seem impossible to save. Part of this is that he often plays as a "sweeper-keeper," stepping out of the goal to help defend against opposing players.

- **Gianluigi Buffon:** Another legendary goalkeeper, Gianluigi Buffon, is renowned for his leadership and reliability. He isn't afraid to dive into tough situations, even colliding with opposing players' feet if necessary, which shows just how tough you need to be to be a goalkeeper!

Defenders

Defenders are like the safety net for the team. They work hard to stop the opposing players from getting to the goal. Here's how they're organized:

Center-backs (CB)

Center-backs are the defensive linemen of soccer who stand tall in the middle of the field and do whatever it takes to keep attackers at bay. Their job is to block opposing players and clear the ball from danger, which makes them the backbone of the team's defense.

They must be quick on their feet, ready to tackle or intercept passes, and anticipate where the ball is going. If you watch any of Virgil van Dijk's or Antonio Rudiger's matches, their qualities are exactly what you want to emulate: an uncanny ability to read the game, as well as physical strength with lightning-fast reactions.

When things get tense, and the opposing team is pressing hard, center-backs are the ones who step up. They need to be decisive and powerful in their clearances—whether a well-timed header or a booming kick up the field.

A solid center-back is also a great communicator. They direct their teammates, ensuring everyone knows their roles and responsibilities, especially during set pieces like corners and free kicks. Then, once they've won the ball, they can send accurate passes to midfielders or even launch long balls to forwards.

Full-Backs (RB/LB)

Full-backs are the players on the left and right flanks of the field, and they have a unique job that blends defense and attack. They're responsible for defending against speedy wingers, using their agility and quickness to keep those attackers in check. If you've seen Andrew Robertson or Joao Cancelo play, you know how effective they are at shutting down the opponent's offense.

But it's not just about defense! Full-backs also join the attack whenever possible. They make overlapping runs to support wingers, creating extra options for offensive plays. Once they push up the field, they can deliver key crosses into the box, setting up scoring opportunities.

Sweeper (SW)

The sweeper isn't as common in today's game because teams now focus more on attacking and ball possession. Positioned behind the center-backs, the sweeper is there to catch any threats that slip through.

For example, during the 1998 World Cup, Frank de Boer was a key sweeper for the Dutch team. He would cover for the center-backs and step in to intercept passes, making sure attackers didn't have easy chances.

When an opponent breaks through, the sweeper must step up and clear the ball. Good sweepers are also leaders who communicate with the center-backs to keep everyone organized.

Midfielders

Midfielders are the link between defense and offense. They help control the pace of the game and keep possession of the ball. Here's what they do:

Central Midfielders (CM)

As someone who's played the central midfield position, I can tell you it's like being the heart of the team. Central midfielders are often referred to as the engine because we're the ones connecting defense and attack. Our job is to distribute the ball and control the game's tempo.

When you get the ball, it's your job to make quick decisions. You're constantly scanning the field, looking for teammates making runs or finding space, whether it's a short pass to keep possession or a long ball to catch the defense off guard; every touch counts.

I remember a match where I received the ball near the halfway line, saw our striker making a run behind their defenders, and played a perfectly timed through ball. It sliced through the defense, and our striker latched onto it, just managing to slot it past the keeper. The thrill of seeing that pass lead to a goal is what makes this position so rewarding.

Remember, if you're in this position, you need to watch the flow of the game closely. If the team is under pressure, you might need to slow things down and play safe passes to regain composure. On the flip side, when you're in a good rhythm, it's time to push the tempo, looking to exploit gaps in the opponent's defense. It's all about reading the game and knowing when to speed up or slow down.

Central midfielders aren't just about attack; we also have to track back and help defend. A trick that helps is to position yourself at a slight angle when marking an opponent. This way, you can see the ball and their body language at the same time. Also, try to keep your hands behind your back. This makes you less likely to commit a foul and keeps your body ready to react quickly.

Attacking Midfielders (CAM)

Attacking midfielders (CAM) are positioned closer to the opponent's goal, and their focus is on creating scoring opportunities.

A crucial trick in this role is to find pockets of space between defenders. Instead of sticking to the same spot, constantly move to areas where you can receive the ball without being marked. This means reading the defense—if a defender shifts to cover another player, slip into the space they just vacated.

Another key tactic is to use quick one-twos (or wall passes) with your teammates. This not only helps you get around defenders but also creates confusion in their marking. For example, if you receive the ball, quickly pass it to a nearby player and immediately make a run to receive it back in stride.

This kind of movement can catch defenders off guard and open up lanes for a shot on goal. Lastly, don't underestimate the power of feints and changes of pace. A simple head fake or sudden acceleration can create just enough separation to make a decisive pass or take a shot.

Defensive Midfielders (CDM)

Defensive midfielders (CDM) work to disrupt the other team's plays and protect the defense. One useful trick is to anticipate the other team's movements. Pay attention to how they pass and who they tend to favor. By knowing their patterns, you can position yourself in the right spots to cut off their passing options.

It's also effective to apply pressure without diving into tackles. When an opponent receives the ball, close them down quickly but stay balanced. This forces them to make hurried decisions, which can lead to mistakes. Make sure to communicate with your teammates—let your center-backs know if someone is making a run behind them.

When you win the ball, don't just kick it away. Take a moment to look up and find a teammate who will be in a good position to help move the play forward. Look for someone who is making a run or is open in space; they might be able to take advantage of the gap you've just created.

Forwards

Forwards are primarily responsible for scoring goals. They're often the players fans watch closely. Here's their breakdown:

Strikers (ST)

Strikers are the central figures on the pitch and the team's go-to players for scoring goals. Their main job? Put that ball in the net! Think of them as the team's offensive powerhouse. To be a good striker, you need a mix of speed, strength, and some serious technical skills. It's all about outsmarting and outpacing defenders to get those golden scoring opportunities.

Strikers come in different flavors. Some are like goal-hungry poachers, always ready to pounce on any loose balls—think of players like Gary Lineker or Michael Owen, who always seemed to be in the right spot to score. Then there are those who play the target role, using their strength to hold off defenders and set up chances for their teammates, like Harry Kane or Romelu Lukaku.

Wingers (RW/LW)

Wingers are the players on the left and right flanks who bring speed and flair to the game. Their main job is to zip past defenders and deliver those sweet crosses into the box for teammates to score. Think of them as the game's wide playmakers, always looking to stretch the defense and create opportunities.

These players are all about one-on-one matchups, using their quick feet and agility to take on defenders. When you watch someone like Mohamed Salah or Sadio Mané, you can see how they can blow past a guy and whip in a perfect cross or even take a shot themselves. They've got to have great dribbling skills and be able to deliver precise passes while making smart runs.

Wingers are essential to a team's attack. They keep the pressure on the opposition, making it hard for defenders to focus on just one player.

Understanding the Game Flow

Knowing these positions helps you appreciate how the game unfolds. Here are a few key aspects to consider:

- **Formation:** The arrangement of players (like 4-4-2 or 4-3-3) influences the team's strategy and how they interact on the field.
- **Transitions:** The shift from defense to offense happens quickly, often initiated by midfielders who drive the ball forward.
- **Pressing:** Some teams apply pressure to win the ball back quickly, while others may take a more cautious approach, allowing the opponent to hold the ball before striking back.

Each player's role contributes to the overall success of the team, and when everyone plays their part well, it can lead to some thrilling moments on the field.

BASIC SOCCER RULES AND REGULATIONS

Understanding soccer's essential rules is key to playing effectively and with good sportsmanship. Here's a simple breakdown to help you get a better grasp of the game.

Game Structure

A soccer match consists of two 45-minute halves, with a 15-minute break in between. If needed, additional time—called **injury time** or **stoppage time**—is added to each half to make up for any delays due to injuries or substitutions. The game starts with a **kick-off**, decided by a coin toss. The winning team chooses to either start with the ball or pick which goal they'll attack first.

Scoring

Scoring is simple: a team earns a goal when the ball completely crosses the goal line between the posts and beneath the crossbar. Each goal is worth one point. The team with the most points at the end wins. If the match ends in a tie, the competition's rules will decide if it goes to extra time or a penalty shootout.

Referees and Officials

The game is controlled by a referee, who enforces the rules. Two assistant referees help with decisions like offsides, fouls, or when the ball is out of play. In higher-level games, you may also see a fourth official and VAR (Video Assistant Referee) to review critical calls.

Common Fouls and Offenses

Understanding fouls is important for fair play. The offside rule is one of the trickiest: a player is offside if they're closer to the opponent's goal than both the ball and the second-last defender when the ball is passed unless they're in their own half or level with the defender.

Handball is another common offense where players (except goalkeepers in their box) can't deliberately use their hands or arms to control the ball. Accidental handballs are usually not penalized unless they lead to a goal or clear advantage. Physical fouls, like tripping, pushing, or dangerous play, can result in free kicks, penalty kicks, or even yellow or red cards for more serious infractions.

Restarts and Set Pieces

After a foul or when the ball goes out of play, the game restarts in various ways:

- **Free kicks:** For less serious fouls, a free kick is awarded. It can be direct (shot directly at the goal) or indirect (must touch another player before scoring).
- **Penalty kicks:** For serious fouls in the penalty area, the attacking team gets a penalty shot from 12 yards out, with only the goalkeeper to beat.
- **Throw-ins:** When the ball crosses the touchline, the opposing team throws it back into play using both hands, keeping both feet on the ground.

- **Goal kicks:** When the ball crosses the goal line but isn't a goal and is last touched by an attacker, the defending team kicks it from their goal area.
- **Corner kicks:** If a defender last touches the ball before it goes over the goal line, the attacking team gets a corner kick from the nearest corner.

Player Positions and Roles

Each position in soccer has unique responsibilities. Whether you're a fast winger, a creative midfielder, or a strong defender, understanding these roles helps you find where you fit best on the team. Recognizing how each position contributes to the overall strategy can make you a smarter, more effective player.

Soccer is all about teamwork. Every player, from the goalkeeper to the striker, has an important role to play. By understanding your strengths and how they contribute to the team's success, you can improve not just your game but your entire soccer experience. Dive into your role with confidence, and bring your best every time you step onto the field!

CHAPTER 2:

ESSENTIAL SKILLS AND TECHNIQUES

Do you know the difference between a volley and a side-foot shot? What about how to maintain steady control of the ball? The premise behind soccer—running around kicking a ball—may seem simple enough, but don't let that fool you. There's a lot of technical know-how to learn if you want to make the most of the game.

I often advise people who love soccer but don't have much experience to study the basics. You can learn a lot by watching the greats do their thing, but if you combine that with the observations and explanations you'll find in a book, you'll be a step ahead.

By the end of this chapter, you'll understand many fundamental skills and techniques—like dribbling, passing, shooting, and defending—giving you a solid foundation to build your game. Whether you're playing for fun or looking to get serious, mastering these basics is key to becoming a more confident and skilled player.

PASSING AND RECEIVING TECHNIQUES

Whether you're setting up a game-winning assist or simply keeping possession, mastering these skills is non-negotiable. You might have the footwork of Messi, but without precision in passing or control in receiving, the ball won't stay with you long. This section dives deep into the crucial techniques that will turn you into a player who can move the ball like a pro while controlling your team.

Basic Pass Types

Each pass has a purpose, and knowing when to use each one is critical to your success on the field.

Short Passes

These are the bread and butter of your game. Short, quick passes maintain possession and keep the ball moving within tight spaces.

- **Execution tip:** Use the inside of your foot, which offers the most surface area and control. Your plant foot should point in the direction you want the ball to go, and the passing leg should swing through smoothly.
- **When to use it:** Short passes are ideal when you're under pressure and need to keep the ball in close quarters or when playing midfield triangles to draw opponents in.

Long Passes

Long balls cover larger distances or switch play from one side of the field to the other. This can catch the opposition off guard, opening up space for your team.

- **Execution tip:** Strike the ball with the instep of your foot (laces) and follow through. A good long pass requires balance, so plant your foot firmly and maintain your body's stability.
- **When to use it:** You need to switch the field or send a teammate on a fast break. These passes bypass midfield congestion and quickly move the ball into attacking areas.

Through Passes

Through balls are designed to split the defense and set up your teammates for a goal-scoring opportunity.

- **Execution tip:** Timing is everything. The ball should be passed into space for your teammate to run onto. Use the inside of your foot for accuracy, and aim just ahead of the runner.
- **When to use it:** Ideal when you spot your teammate making a run behind the defenders. It's all about precision, threading the ball between defenders without overhitting it.

Recognizing when to use each pass type can make or break your team's performance. A misjudged long ball or an ill-timed through pass could result in a turnover, while a perfectly executed pass puts your team in a scoring position.

Receiving the Ball

Passing is only half the battle—receiving the ball is equally important. To keep possession and set up your next move, you need to receive the ball with finesse.

Proper Body Positioning

Your body position when receiving the ball can make all the difference. Position yourself so you can see the ball and the field, giving you a better understanding of where to direct your next move.

- **Execution tip:** Always open your body up to the field, which means angling yourself to face where the ball is coming from and where you want to go next. This allows for a quick turn or pass.

Soft Touches for Control

The softer your first touch, the better control you'll have over the ball. A heavy touch can result in a turnover, especially when under pressure from defenders.

- **Execution tip:** Cushion the ball using the inside of your foot or even the outside when necessary. The key is to receive the ball gently so it stays close, setting up your next move instantly.

Read the Ball's Trajectory!

Learning to read how the ball is coming toward you helps you decide whether to receive it with your chest, thigh, or feet.

- **Execution tip:** If the ball is high, adjust your body accordingly—chest it down or trap it with your thigh. If it's fast and low, be prepared to use the inside of your foot to cushion the impact.

Good receiving techniques allow you to maintain possession and dictate the flow of the game. With the right positioning and soft touch, you can control the tempo, create space, and eliminate unnecessary turnovers.

Passing Drills

Now that you know how to pass and receive, it's time to put those skills into practice. Engaging drills can transform your passing from something you think about into second nature.

Triangle Passing Drill

Set up three cones in a triangle and have players pass the ball between them, focusing on quick, short passes and movement off the ball.

- **Why it works:** This drill helps you improve your short passing accuracy and quick decision-making, as well as movement, to support your teammates after the pass.

Long Ball Switch Drill

Players stand on opposite sides of the field, practicing long balls to one another, aiming for accuracy and distance.

- **Why it works:** It builds your long passing ability and ensures you can switch the play quickly and accurately during games.

Through Ball Drill

Two attackers play against two defenders in a tight space, practicing through balls and running into space.

- **Why it works:** This simulates game-like situations, helping you develop timing and accuracy in your through passes.

COMMUNICATION IN PASSING

Passing is about technique as much as it's about communication. Verbal and non-verbal cues help your team work together seamlessly, ensuring that passes land where they're supposed to.

Verbal Communication

Calling for the ball is more than shouting "Here!" It's about giving clear, precise instructions to your teammates.

- **Execution tip:** Use phrases like "Man on!" (to signal pressure from an opponent) or "Time!" (to let them know they're unmarked). This communication creates trust and efficiency in play.

Non-Verbal Cues

Sometimes, you won't have time to shout, and that's where non-verbal communication comes in.

- **Execution tip:** Eye contact with a teammate or a quick hand gesture can be enough to signal where you want the ball. The best teams understand each other without needing to say a word.

Effective communication fosters strong team dynamics. Knowing where your teammates are—and where they want the ball—ensures that passes are sharp and effective. Practicing communication during training will make passing feel intuitive on the field.

Dribbling Fundamentals

Whether driving down the wing or weaving through a packed defense, dribbling allows you to move the ball while maintaining control, setting up chances, or creating space for teammates. In this section, we'll break down the core principles of dribbling and show how it can be your secret weapon in different game scenarios.

Basic Dribbling Techniques

Dribbling isn't one-size-fits-all. Each situation on the field calls for a different dribbling style. Learning when and how to use various techniques will make you a dynamic threat in any game.

Straight-Line Dribbling

This is the simplest form of dribbling, where you maintain control of the ball while running in a straight line. It's all about speed and keeping the ball close.

- **Execution tip:** Use the top of your foot (laces) to gently tap the ball forward as you run. Keep your stride smooth and your touches light to ensure the ball stays within reach.

- **When to use it:** Ideal when you have open space ahead of you, like breaking through the midfield or sprinting down the wing.

Lateral Dribbling

Lateral dribbling involves moving the ball side to side, often to avoid defenders or change direction quickly.

- **Execution tip:** Use the inside and outside of your feet to push the ball from side to side while keeping your balance. Stay low and keep your knees slightly bent to enhance agility.
- **When to use it:** Best when trying to beat a defender in tight spaces or looking to reposition yourself for a better pass or shot.

Feints and Fakes

Feints, like stepovers or body swerves, are designed to mislead the defender into thinking you're going one way when you're going the other.

- **Execution tip:** Use quick, deceptive movements with your body—such as a shoulder drop or a step over the ball—to trick the defender. Practice selling the fake with your whole body to make it convincing.
- **When to use it:** These moves are great in one-on-one situations when you need to get past a defender or create space for a pass.

Understanding which dribbling style to use in different contexts will optimize your approach against defenders. For instance, lateral dribbling helps you escape tight spaces, while feints are key in 1v1 situations. The ability to switch between these techniques during a game makes you unpredictable and harder to defend against.

And remember: speed changes can unbalance defenders—accelerating quickly after a feint can be the difference between getting past your marker or losing the ball.

Footwork and Ball Control

Great dribblers, like Lionel Messi or Marta, aren't just fast—they're masters of close control. Footwork and ball control are crucial for keeping the ball within your grasp while evading defenders.

Low Body Posture and Balance

When dribbling, keeping a low center of gravity helps you stay balanced and agile. Quick footwork combined with a slightly crouched posture gives you better control over the ball and makes sudden changes in direction easier.

- **Execution tip:** Bend your knees and stay low to the ground. This will allow you to shift your weight more quickly, making it easier to move left, right, or stop suddenly.

Close Control

Keeping the ball close to your feet is key when dribbling in tight spaces or under pressure from defenders. The closer the ball is, the less likely it will be stolen.

- **Execution tip:** Use soft touches with both the inside and outside of your feet to keep the ball within inches of you. Short, rapid touches allow for quicker turns and better evasion.

Using Both Feet

To be a truly versatile player, you need to be able to dribble effectively with both feet. If you're only comfortable with your dominant foot, you'll become predictable to defenders.

- **Execution tip:** Practice drills where you alternate touches between your left and right foot. Start slow, then increase your speed as you become more comfortable with your weaker foot.

Good footwork allows you to keep the ball out of your opponent's reach, even in the most crowded parts of the field. Developing your non-dominant foot for dribbling increases your versatility in attack and helps you outwit defenders who may assume you'll favor one side.

Situations

Dribbling in one-on-one situations is often the make-or-break moment in a game. Knowing how to approach these duels can give you a massive advantage.

Analyze Your Opponent

A successful 1v1 depends on how well you read your defender. Pay attention to their body language—are they lunging forward? Flat-footed? Hesitant? Use that to your advantage.

- **Execution tip:** If the defender is off-balance or overcommitting, that's your cue to strike. A quick cut or acceleration can send them the wrong way.

Quick Decision-Making

In one-on-one situations, split-second decisions are essential. Whether you decide to dribble past your defender or pass the ball, the longer you hesitate, the longer the defender has to stop you.

- **Execution tip:** Keep your eyes up and be decisive. Choose your move early—whether it's a feint, change of direction, or burst of speed—and commit to it fully.

1v1 scenarios are common in soccer, especially in attacking situations. Being confident in these moments can lead to game-changing breakthroughs. Practicing these skills in training will build your confidence when the pressure's on during the game.

Avoiding Defenders

To dribble successfully, you must know how to evade defenders without losing control of the ball. This is where body movement and field awareness come into play.

Fakes and Body Feints

The best way to beat a defender is to convince them you're going one way when you're going the other. Body feints are small movements that cause defenders to commit prematurely.

- **Execution tip:** Use your shoulders, hips, and eyes to "sell" your fake. Even a subtle shoulder drop or glance in the wrong direction can make a defender think you're about to go that way, giving you the chance to cut in the opposite direction.

Keeping Your Head Up

Dribbling with your head down limits your field of vision and awareness. By keeping your head up, you can see defenders closing in and spot-open teammates for a pass or a shooting opportunity.

- **Execution tip:** Practice dribbling with your head up by doing drills that encourage scanning the field while keeping the ball under control, like dribbling around cones while focusing on your surroundings.

Evasive Maneuvers

If you're being closed down by multiple defenders, quick, evasive movements can help you maintain possession. Sharp cuts, quick turns, and acceleration will help you escape tight situations.

- **Execution tip:** Use moves like the Cruyff Turn or stepovers to deceive defenders. Quick pivots and sudden changes in direction can open up space to continue your attack.

In soccer, it's not enough to just dribble—the real magic happens when you evade defenders and create space for yourself and your teammates. Learning these evasive techniques gives you the upper hand in attack, increasing your chances of creating goal-scoring opportunities.

Dribbling isn't just about flashy moves but control, balance, and smart decision-making. Regardless of whether you're going head-to-head with a defender or looking to create space for a pass, these foundational dribbling skills will help you move around the field like a pro, enhancing both your individual performance and your team's.

SHOOTING ACCURACY AND POWER

Regarding soccer, scoring goals is the ultimate aim, and the two key elements of goal-scoring are accuracy and power. Whether you're blasting a shot from outside the box or placing a finesse shot past the goalkeeper, mastering these aspects of shooting will make you a lethal threat on the field.

Think of Cristiano Ronaldo's iconic free kick against Portsmouth in 2008. That goal was the perfect combination of power and precision. Ronaldo struck the ball with such force and accuracy that it curled into the top corner, leaving the goalkeeper with no chance. His ability to control both elements in his shot made him a scoring machine, and mastering these skills can do the same for you. This section breaks down the mechanics, drills, and mindset you'll need.

The Mechanics Behind the Perfect Shot

It goes without saying that there's more to shooting than just kicking the ball as hard as you can. Proper technique is what separates average shots from world-class strikes. Learning the mechanics of various shooting styles will help you develop power and precision.

Instep Drive (Laces)

This technique is ideal when you want maximum power. It's often used for long-range shots or when you're trying to blast the ball past the goalkeeper.

- **Execution tip:** Use your laces (instep) to strike the ball. Keep your body leaning slightly forward, plant your non-kicking foot next to the ball, and follow through with your kicking leg for a powerful shot.
- **When to use it:** Great for shots from a distance or when you have time to wind up for a big strike.

Volley

A volley is when you strike the ball before it touches the ground. It requires timing and precision but can lead to spectacular goals.

- **Execution tip:** Keep your eyes on the ball and time your strike as it's coming down. For power, use the top of your foot, and for placement, you can use the inside of your foot.
- **When to use it:** When a cross or a loose ball comes to you in midair, and there's no time to bring it down before shooting.

Side-Foot Shot

If you're looking for accuracy rather than power, the side-foot shot is your best option. It's used to place the ball into specific areas of the goal.

- **Execution tip:** Strike the ball with the inside of your foot. Open up your body and aim to place the shot where the goalkeeper can't reach it.
- **When to use it:** Ideal for close-range shots when you need to place the ball into a corner or past a charging goalkeeper.

From your foot positioning to your follow-through, each part of the process is essential for combining power and accuracy. Practicing different shooting methods will prepare you for various in-game situations, whether it's a booming long shot or a delicate tap-in.

Where to Aim and Why It Matters

Scoring goals isn't just about hitting the target—it's about knowing where to place the ball to make it difficult for the goalkeeper to save. Learning how to analyze the keeper's positioning and target the right areas of the goal will boost your scoring chances.

Reading the Goalkeeper

Before taking a shot, it's crucial to take a quick look at the goalkeeper. Are they leaning to one side? Standing too far off their line? Identifying these cues can give you an idea of where to aim. If the keeper is positioned too far to one side, aim for the far corner. If they're off their line, a chip shot over their head could do the trick.

Target Zones

Dividing the goal into target zones (top corners, bottom corners, near post, far post) will help you focus your shots. The corners are the most difficult areas for goalkeepers to reach, making them prime targets. Regularly practicing shooting into the top corners or low into the bottom corners will develop muscle memory and improve precision.

Shooting Under Pressure

In a game, you rarely have the luxury of time. Training to shoot accurately and quickly under pressure will improve your in-game performance.

Work on drills that force you to shoot with defenders closing in or after a quick pass. The faster you can get your shot off, the more effective you'll be.

Shooting Drills

To become a top scorer, you need to practice your shooting until it becomes second nature. Drills that replicate game scenarios will help you develop both accuracy and power while improving your ability to react under pressure.

Overhead and Side-Foot Shots Drill

Set up targets in different zones of the goal (cones, small nets, or even hanging objects) and practice shooting from various distances, alternating between side-foot placement shots and powerful overhead strikes.

- **Why it works:** This drill helps diversify your shooting ability so you can score in any situation—whether it's placing a shot in the corner or powering one from outside the box.

Shooting Drill

Have a teammate or coach act as a goalkeeper. Receive a pass, take a touch, and then shoot while under pressure from the oncoming "keeper."

- **Why it works:** This drill simulates in-game scenarios where you'll have to shoot quickly and with a defender or keeper closing in. It improves both composure and shooting under pressure.

Shooting While Dribbling Drill

Set up cones in a line, dribble through them at speed, and take a shot at the goal at the end. Aim for specific target zones in the goal.

- **Why it works:** This drill helps you practice shooting after dribbling, a common scenario in games. It improves ball control, balance, and shooting accuracy after a burst of movement.

Shooting drills help you build muscle memory, making your shots instinctive in games. By practicing different shot types and introducing elements of competition or pressure, you'll be better prepared to take your chances when they come.

Staying Cool Under Pressure

Shooting isn't just about physical skill—it's also a mental game. Being able to stay composed in high-pressure moments can be the difference between hitting the target or missing entirely. Developing mental resilience and confidence will elevate your shooting to the next level.

Visualization

Before taking a shot, imagine the ball hitting the back of the net. Visualization can boost your confidence and improve focus.

- **Execution tip:** Close your eyes for a moment and picture the exact shot you want to take. Visualize the ball going into the corner of the goal, past the keeper's outstretched hands.

Relaxation Techniques

When the pressure is on, it's easy to tense up. Teaching yourself to stay relaxed will help you execute cleaner, more controlled shots.

- **Execution tip:** Take a deep breath before striking the ball. Focus on your technique rather than the outcome, and trust your abilities.

Post-Shot Analysis

Whether you score or miss, it's important to reflect on your shot. What went well? What could you improve? This reflection helps build continuous improvement.

- **Execution tip:** After each game or training session, take a few minutes to mentally review your shots. Analyze your technique, decision-making, and mindset. This will help you correct mistakes and replicate successful shots.

In high-stakes moments—whether it's a penalty kick or a last-minute shot to win the game—mental composure can be the deciding factor. By practicing visualization and relaxation techniques, you'll improve your ability to focus and execute under pressure. Reflecting on your shots will lead to continuous improvement, building confidence for future opportunities.

Shooting with accuracy and power is the key to becoming a prolific goal-scorer. By mastering various shooting techniques, aiming for specific target zones, and practicing through engaging drills, you'll be able to strike the ball with both confidence and precision. Add a strong mental approach to shooting, and you'll be ready to handle high-pressure situations with ease. Keep practicing, stay composed, and before you know it, you'll be hitting the back of the net like a pro.

BASIC DEFENDING SKILLS

Defending is just as important as scoring goals. A strong defender can turn the tide of a game, preventing the opponent from finding the back of the net and giving your team the foundation to launch counterattacks. This section covers the essential defensive skills you need to master to become a reliable player that your team can count on.

Fundamentals of Positioning

The foundation of great defense is knowing where to be on the field at all times. Effective positioning ensures that you can anticipate your opponent's movements, cut off passing lanes, and block shots.

Correct Body Angles

Defenders need to position their bodies in a way that makes it harder for attackers to get past them or deliver a clean pass. The right body angle forces the attacker into less dangerous areas of the field.

- **Execution tip:** Stand side-on to the opponent, facing slightly toward the ball. This will allow you to block their path to goal while being ready to intercept a pass.
- **Why it works:** Forcing attackers into less threatening areas reduces the chances of them making a dangerous play.

Watching Both the Ball and the Opponent

Being aware of the ball is important, but so is keeping an eye on the opponent you're marking. You need to find a balance between watching the play unfold and staying ready to stop the attacker.

- **Execution tip:** Keep your head on a swivel. Glance between the ball and your opponent, using your peripheral vision to stay aware of both.
- **Why it works:** Defending isn't just reacting; it's anticipating the next move. Watching both the ball and your opponent ensures you're always in a position to react.

Predictive Movement

The best defenders can often predict what the attacker will do next. Anticipating a pass or a move can help you step in and break up the play before it develops.

- **Execution tip:** Focus on reading the attacker's body language. Are they looking to pass? Preparing to cut inside? Use these cues to anticipate their next move and react accordingly.

- **Why it works:** Defensive awareness is about more than being quick—it's about being one step ahead. Predictive movement allows you to intercept plays and gain control.

Proper positioning is the bedrock of any strong defense. In maintaining correct angles, staying aware of both the ball and player and practicing predictive movement, you'll be able to cut off attacks before they become threats.

Tackling Techniques

Done correctly, tackling allows you to win back possession and shut down attacking threats. Done poorly, it leads to fouls, free kicks, or worse, penalties. Learning the proper technique is essential.

Standing Tackle

A standing tackle is the most common way to win the ball back. It requires precise timing and a strong stance.

- **Execution tip:** Get low, bend your knees, and time your tackle for when the attacker's touch is heavy or the ball is exposed. Use your foot to sweep the ball away cleanly.
- **When to use it:** Perfect for when you're close to the attacker and can challenge them for the ball directly.

Sliding Tackle

Sliding tackles are riskier but can be effective in certain situations. Timing and technique are critical to avoid fouls.

- **Execution tip:** Approach the attacker at an angle, extend your leg, and use the inside of your foot to sweep the ball away. Be sure to get the ball first to avoid giving away a foul.
- **When to use it:** Use sliding tackles when you're in a last-ditch situation or need to block a shot or cross.

Quick Recovery

After a tackle, especially a sliding one, it's important to get back on your feet quickly to continue defending.

- **Execution tip:** Practice getting up swiftly after hitting the ground. Keep your body low and use your hands to push yourself back into position.
- **Why it works:** Recovery speed can make or break a defender. The quicker you're back on your feet, the quicker you're ready to win the ball again.

With enough practice, you'll develop the ability to win the ball cleanly and avoid unnecessary fouls. The faster you recover after a tackle, the more prepared you are for the next phase of play.

Marking the Opponent

Marking is the bread and butter of defense. If you look at Paolo Maldini, one of the greatest defenders of all time, you'll see how mastering marking can completely shut down even the most dangerous attackers. In the 1994 Champions League final,

Maldini marked Barcelona's Romário so tightly that he rarely touched the ball the entire game!

Man-To-Man Marking

In this approach, you're tasked with staying close to a specific player, ensuring they have little space or time to operate.

- **Execution tip:** Stay close enough to your opponent to challenge them for the ball, but not so close that they can easily turn you. Focus on positioning yourself between them and the goal.
- **When to use it:** Best when you're assigned to neutralize a specific player, such as a dangerous striker or playmaker.

Zone Marking

In zone marking, instead of sticking to one player, you defend an area of the field, reacting to whoever enters your zone.

- **Execution tip:** Be aware of the players around you, but don't follow them out of your zone. Communicate with your teammates to ensure no one is left unmarked when attackers move between zones.
- **When to use it:** Ideal for set pieces or defending in a compact block when the opposition is trying to break through your lines.

Denying Space

A key part of marking is denying your opponent time and space to control the ball. The closer you stay, the less room they have to make a play.

- **Execution tip:** Stay tight, but give yourself enough room to react if they try to make a move. If they receive the ball, challenge them immediately before they can turn or pass.
- **Why it works:** Denying space makes it difficult for attackers to control the ball or create scoring opportunities. The less time they have, the more likely they are to make mistakes.

Effective marking, whether man-to-man or zone, limits the opponent's ability to get on the ball and make plays. By practicing these techniques, you'll become a constant presence that attackers struggle to shake off, making you an essential part of your team's defense.

Building a Defensive Unit

Defense is not just an individual effort; it's a team responsibility. Clear communication is critical to ensuring that everyone knows their role, especially when organizing the backline or reacting to attacks.

Calling Out Directions

As a defender, you need to be vocal. Whether it's telling your teammate to cover a space or warning them of an approaching attacker, clear communication helps prevent defensive breakdowns.

- **Execution tip:** Use simple, clear commands like "man on" (when an attacker is closing in), "push up" (to move the defensive line forward), or "switch" (to pass off an opponent to a teammate).

- **Why it works:** Quick, effective communication keeps the entire defensive line on the same page, preventing gaps or confusion that attackers could exploit.

Alerting Teammates

Sometimes, defenders need to play the role of the eyes in the back of their teammates' heads. Alerting them to dangers they might not see can save your team from conceding a goal.

- **Execution tip:** Call out when an opponent is running into open space or when your teammate is being pressured from behind. Always keep the communication clear and loud.
- **Why it works:** Teammates rely on your awareness as much as their own. By alerting them to danger, you prevent mistakes and close off attacking options for the opposition.

Practicing Communication

Like any other skill, communication needs to be practiced. Running drills that require defenders to talk to each other will improve your unit's cohesion.

- **Execution tip:** In training, run small-sided games where the focus is on defensive communication. Make communication a key part of every defensive drill.
- **Why it works:** A well-communicated defense is much harder to break down. The more you practice, the more natural these conversations will become during a match.

Defending is about teamwork, and teamwork requires communication. When defenders talk to each other on the field, they can see trouble coming before it even happens, react fast, and stay in sync. Without that teamwork, even the best defenders can get caught off guard. Clear, constant communication turns your defense from a group of individuals into a rock-solid wall no one can break through.

CHAPTER 3:
ADVANCED SKILL DEVELOPMENT

Imagine if there were a playbook that could unlock every skill you need to dominate the field—well, this is it. In this book, I've gathered the techniques I've seen (and used) to turn ordinary players into game-changers, organized into two levels: basic and advanced.

In the first two chapters, you nailed the essentials. Without those, you'd be stumbling through the game and probably getting booed off the pitch. But now, it's time to level up. In this chapter, you'll learn the skills that will elevate you from just another player to the one everyone's watching.

Remember: reading isn't enough. Practice these moves until they're automatic and you can execute them in your sleep. If you're coaching a team, make sure the basics are rock solid before unleashing these advanced skills—mastery is key, and the last thing you want is confusion slowing your progress.

BODY TRAPPING TECHNIQUES

You can't catch the ball in soccer, but you can stop its motion by trapping it. Different parts of your body are suited for different kinds of ball traps, and understanding this will give you versatility in any situation:

Feet

The foot is the most commonly used part for trapping the ball, but there's nuance here. When the ball is coming at you on the ground, you aim to cushion it. Instead of stopping the ball dead with a flat foot, you should *pull back slightly* upon contact to absorb the ball's speed. This is called a *soft touch*. The key is to ensure the ball stays close, within a step of your foot, so that you can make your next move instantly.

Thighs

When the ball comes in at mid-height, use your thigh to control it. The key here is not letting the ball bounce off; you need to meet it gently, absorbing its energy by slightly lowering your thigh upon impact. It's almost like letting the ball *sink* into your leg. Get the angle wrong, and the ball will shoot in unpredictable directions. Get it right, and the ball drops neatly at your feet, ready for action.

Chest

High balls require control of your chest. Similar to thigh trapping, you need to cushion the ball rather than just stop it. Lean back slightly as the ball comes in, creating a curved surface to land on. Your chest naturally absorbs the ball's energy, allowing it to fall straight down, where you can quickly move into your next action. This method is great for long passes or goal kicks that need instant control in crowded situations.

Every part of your body becomes a tool for controlling the ball when you adjust your positioning correctly. By learning to adjust your body angle—leaning back for chest control, angling your foot for ground traps, or raising your knee for thigh traps—you can gain total mastery over the ball.

FOOTWORK DRILLS FOR CONTROL

Now, how do you *train* for this level of precision? It all comes down to footwork drills that build muscle memory and sharpen your reflexes. Here are a few specific drills to help develop your ball control:

Cone Dribbling With Traps

Set up cones in a zigzag pattern and pass the ball to a teammate, who plays it back to you at different heights (low, mid, high). As the ball comes in, use different body parts to trap it—feet, thighs, or chest—before continuing to dribble through the cones. This drill forces you to adjust on the fly, much like in a real game.

First Touch Circuits

In this drill, a coach or teammate passes you the ball at various speeds and angles. Your task is to trap the ball with a *single soft touch* and return it immediately. Vary the passes—ground balls, bouncing passes, and aerial balls—to build confidence in controlling the ball under any condition. This drill sharpens your ability to react quickly and maintain balance, which is crucial for staying composed when an opponent is closing in.

Wall Pass Control

Pass the ball against a wall and trap it as it rebounds unpredictably. The focus is on quick feet *and* soft touches. As you improve, increase the speed of your passes to the wall to simulate the faster pace of an actual match.

These drills emphasize the importance of balance and body control. A strong foundation of footwork helps you maintain control, especially when the ball takes unexpected bounces. Light touches and good reaction times become second nature, allowing you to control the ball with precision.

USING SPACE AND TIME

The best players aren't just great at trapping the ball—they know exactly *when* and *where* to trap it. Space and time are your two most valuable assets, and how you manage them can dictate the game's flow. Here's how to maximize both:

Anticipating Ball Trajectories

As you approach the ball, you must assess the space around you. Is a defender closing in? Is there open space to turn into after the trap? The best players constantly scan the field before receiving the ball, so they already know their next move before the ball even reaches them. This spatial awareness allows you to make quicker, smarter decisions.

Positioning Your Body in Space

When trapping the ball, positioning yourself to shield it from the opponent is crucial. If you know a defender is nearby, you should angle your body so they can't easily reach the ball. This buys you extra time to make your next move. Always aim to trap the ball in open space rather than trapping it flat-footed, which can leave you vulnerable.

The ability to control the ball while knowing what's happening around you turns basic trapping into tactical brilliance. You gain not just possession but control of the game's tempo.

OVERCOMING PRESSURE

The real test of your ball control skills comes when you're under pressure. It's easy enough to trap the ball when you've got time and space, but what about when you have a defender breathing down your neck? This is where composure and shielding come into play.

- **Shielding the ball:** When an opponent closes in, your body becomes your shield. Use your arms and body positioning to block the defender from reaching the ball while you control it. For example, if you trap a pass with your foot, immediately place your body between the ball and the defender, angling yourself to keep the ball safe. Mastering this technique allows you to maintain possession even in tight spaces.

- **Composure in high-pressure situations:** One of the hardest skills to develop is keeping calm under pressure. The instinct is to panic when defenders close in, but the key is to keep your touch light and trust your training. Practicing high-pressure drills—like trapping the ball with defenders sprinting at you—can simulate the chaos of a match, helping you develop the composure to hold onto the ball when it counts most.

If you want to take your dribbling to the next level, you've got to think about more than just getting past a defender. It's about how you get past them and set up the next play. Dribbling is where the magic happens on the field—it's that split second where you can leave a defender guessing or, better yet, on the wrong side of the play. Here's how you can make that magic happen.

ADVANCED DRIBBLING MOVES

Feints and Fakes

Nothing feels better than fooling a defender with a good feint—it's like playing chess with your feet, but you're always one move ahead. The trick to a great fake? It's not just about the feet; it's about selling the whole package.

- **Subtle vs. exaggerated fakes:** You've got to know your audience, the defender in front of you. Sometimes, all it takes is a small drop of the shoulder, like you're going one way, and suddenly they're biting hard. *That's when you cut the other way, and they're left in the dust.* Other times, you've got to go bigger—think full step-overs or maybe even a Cruyff turn—something to make them commit. The best dribblers know when to keep it low-key and when to be flashy. You need both tools in your kit.

- **Timing and body language:** This is where the mind games kick in. It's not enough to throw a step over; you must *sell it* with your whole body. Your head, shoulders, and eyes all have to be in sync. If you're faking to the right, make the defender believe you're already halfway there with your body. But the real secret? *Timing.* Do it too early, and the defender has time to recover. Too late, and you're probably getting tackled. The sweet spot is just before they commit—give them that half-second where they think they've read you, and then you cut the other way.

- **Practice against real defenders:** You've got to practice these moves against actual defenders to know what works and what doesn't. When I was learning, nothing was more valuable than going up against teammates in one-on-one drills. You quickly learn what fakes are effective, how fast you need to move, and where to adjust. Make this a habit, and you'll see defenders biting on your moves left and right.

CHANGE OF PACE AND DIRECTION

If you've ever dribbled past someone and felt like you left them in slow motion, you know the power of a good change of pace. It's not just about being fast—it's about knowing when to turn on the jets and when to slow down.

- **Explosive speed:** There's nothing more satisfying than cruising along, luring the defender in, and then, *boom*, a quick burst of speed, and you're gone. It doesn't matter if you're not the fastest player on the field—if you know how to shift gears at the right moment, you'll leave defenders scrambling to catch up. You want to push the ball ahead and then *explode* past them. The key is getting comfortable accelerating out of your dribble, not just sprinting in a straight line but bursting out of a move.

- **Quick feet and agility:** Ever tried to turn a defender inside out with a sharp cut? It's one of the most satisfying feelings in the game. To pull it off, you need quick feet and the ability to change direction on a dime. Think of it like dodging in a crowded room—you've got to plant, cut, and shift your weight without losing speed. Lateral drills, like agility ladders or quick changes between cones, are perfect. When you practice this enough, you can zig-zag through defenders like it's nothing, leaving them flat-footed as you turn them inside out.

- **Real-game situations:** In the game, you don't want to just change direction for the sake of it. The goal is to create space or open up a passing lane. Sometimes, you only need a quick cut to the side to make room for a shot. Other times, a defender might be tight on you, and one sharp change of pace can be all it takes to lose them and drive into the box.

USING BOTH FEET

Let me tell you, being one-footed limits you *big time*. If you're only comfortable dribbling with your dominant foot, defenders will pick up on that quickly. They'll know exactly which way to push you; suddenly, your options shrink. That's why becoming two-footed is a *game-changer*.

- **Ambidextrous dribbling:** The more comfortable you are with both feet, the more unpredictable you become. You can fake left, shift the ball to your right in a heartbeat, or vice versa. It's about giving yourself as many options as possible. If a defender tries to force you to your weak side, you should still be able to go there confidently and beat them.

- **Drills to build proficiency:** One thing I always did was simple, repetitive drills to strengthen my weak foot— cone dribbling, passing, and even juggling, all focusing on the weaker side. The more you push yourself to use it in practice, the more natural it becomes in games. Before you know it, you'll be easily gliding past defenders using both feet.

Creating Space With Dribbling

At the heart of dribbling, it's not just about beating one guy— it's about *creating space* for yourself and your teammates. The best dribblers don't just get past defenders; they manipulate the space around them.

- **When to dribble, when to pass:** You've got to recognize when it's the right time to take a defender on and when it's better to release the ball. If you're in a crowded area, sometimes it's smarter to take one or two touches, draw in defenders, and then *make the pass* to someone in space. But when you choose to dribble, you've got to know how to do it in a way that opens up new options. If you can drag a defender one way and create space on the other side, suddenly, you're not just escaping pressure—you're creating attacking opportunities.

- **Body positioning:** It's not just your feet that create space—it's your whole body. How you shield the ball, position your hips, and angle yourself can buy you the extra second you need to get past someone or set up a teammate. In tight spaces, it's all about keeping the ball close, using your body to protect it, and then exploding into open space when the moment is right.

PRECISION SHOOTING UNDER PRESSURE

Precision shooting under pressure is one of soccer's most thrilling and challenging aspects. It's that heart-pounding moment when the clock is ticking, the defense is closing in, and the goal seems to shrink before you. But this is where champions are made—the ability to stay calm, focus, and hit the back of the net when it matters most. Shooting under pressure isn't just about blasting the ball; it's about accuracy, composure, and decision-making. Here's how you can master it.

Shooting Drills With Variations

To get comfortable scoring under pressure, you must simulate those exact situations in training. It's easy to finish cleanly when you're relaxed, but can you do it when a defender is charging at you or when you've only got a split second to pick your spot?

- **Drills for pressure situations:** One of the best ways to practice shooting under pressure is through drills that force you to make quick decisions. Try a drill where a teammate plays you the ball at random angles—sometimes it's a cross, other times it's a low-driven pass—while another player acts as a defender closing in. You've got to adjust to the ball, decide on your shot in an instant, and fire. These drills build your ability to shoot from various angles and distances, just like you'd face in a game.

- **Target accuracy over power:** This is critical. Under pressure, many players make the mistake of going for pure power, smashing the ball, and hoping for the best. But the reality is, in most game situations, accuracy is what beats the keeper. Focus on hitting the corners—low and hard is often the most effective shot—rather than trying to blast through the goalie. As you get comfortable, you'll notice that the more pressure you're under, the more important placement you become. Drills like target shooting—where small goals or specific spots in the net are your targets—will sharpen this skill.

- **Quick decision-making:** Pressure doesn't just come from defenders or the scoreline—it also comes from having to decide what to do with the ball in a fraction of a second. These drills should push you to make *split-second decisions*. Is it better to take a touch and shoot or strike first time? Should you go near post or far post? The more you train for these quick decisions, the more automatic they'll become in matches. When you're in the moment, you won't overthink—you'll just react.

The Mental Edge in Shooting

Here's the truth: the mental side of shooting is just as important as the physical technique. You could have the best shot in the world, but if your mind isn't right, especially under pressure, you'll miss more than you make. Learning to control your mind can elevate your finishing.

- **Visualization techniques:** Before you even get the ball at your feet, the goal has to be clear in your mind. I've always found that *visualizing* a successful shot before you take it makes a huge difference. Picture the ball hitting the back of the net, see yourself striking it cleanly, and feel that surge of confidence. Visualization helps you stay calm when the pressure is on because, in your mind, you've already scored that goal a hundred times.

- **Positive self-talk:** Confidence is key. Whether you've missed a few chances already or it's your first opportunity, what you tell yourself in those moments matters. Keep your internal dialogue positive: "I've got this," or "Next shot's going in." This kind of *self-talk* will keep your head clear and your confidence high. In practice, make it a habit to talk yourself through tough drills. When you carry this mindset into the game, you'll find yourself much more composed in front of goal.

- **Situational awareness:** The best shooters don't just react to the ball; they anticipate what's going to happen next. Before the ball even gets to you, you should know where the defenders and keeper are and what your best options are. Practice scanning the field, keeping your head up, and *anticipating shooting opportunities* before they open up. The ability to read the game quickly means you're prepared to finish the second that ball arrives.

Finishing Techniques

There's no one-size-fits-all approach to finishing—you've got to have an arsenal of different shooting techniques ready, depending on the situation. It's not always about the textbook strike; sometimes, you must adapt on the fly.

- **Volleys, half-volleys, and driven shots:** Each has its moment in the game, and the more comfortable you are with all of them, the better your finishing will be. For volleys, timing is everything. The ball is coming to you in the air, and you've got to strike it cleanly without overthinking it. Practice striking the ball mid-air to get that crisp connection. Half-volleys, where the ball hits the ground right before you strike it, require a different focus. You need to time your shot perfectly, often with a quick ankle snap to keep the ball low. Driven shots are all about power with precision. This is where your follow-through and foot positioning comes into play. Lean over the ball, drive through it with your laces, and keep your head down to ensure accuracy.

- **Foot positioning and follow-through:** The mechanics matter. When you shoot, where your non-kicking foot is planted and how you follow through make a huge difference. If you're leaning back or off-balance, the shot's going high or wide. Keep your non-kicking foot pointed toward your target, stay low over the ball, and make sure your follow-through is controlled. These fundamentals will help you maintain accuracy, even in tight situations.

- **Player examples:** Think about players like Robert Lewandowski or Harry Kane—two of the best finishers in the game. Lewandowski masters controlling the ball with one touch and finishing with minimal space. Kane's ability to read defenders and get his shot off with perfect placement is second to none. Watch how they position their bodies and prepare for their shots—they're clinical because they combine technique with mental sharpness.

Reacting to Defenders

Shooting with defenders breathing down your neck is the ultimate test. The key here is to stay composed and think one step ahead.

- **Reading defenders:** When a defender closes in, it's all about timing and angle. You've got to read their movements, whether they're diving in for the tackle or jockeying you to force you wide. If they're over-committing, sometimes a quick shift of the ball to the other foot opens up the space you need. If they're trying to block your shot, use them as a screen and bend the ball around them.

- **Body positioning:** One of the best ways to create a shooting chance is by using your body to shield the ball from the defender. Get your body between them and the ball, and use your arms and hips to keep them at bay just long enough to get your shot off. It's not just about brute strength—it's about positioning and balance. Once you've got that down, you can buy yourself that split second you need to pick your spot.

TACKLING AND INTERCEPTION STRATEGIES

Tackling and interceptions are the heartbeat of a solid defense—there's nothing more satisfying than cleanly winning the ball back for your team. It's about more than just stopping an attack; it's about reading the game, anticipating what's coming next, and making split-second decisions to keep your side in control. Whether you're an experienced defender or just learning the ropes, mastering these defensive strategies will not only boost your performance but will also help your team stay strong and cohesive under pressure.

Types of Tackles

Tackling isn't just about diving in and hoping for the best. There's an art to it—a balance between aggression and timing. Knowing which tackle to use and when can be the difference between a game-saving play or giving away a foul in a dangerous area.

- **Slide tackles vs. standing tackles:** These are the two primary types of tackles, and each has its place. A standing tackle is your bread and butter—it's controlled and allows you to stay on your feet, ready to keep moving if necessary. When you're in a tight 1v1 situation or pressing an attacker with nowhere to go, a well-timed standing tackle can win possession without giving up your defensive positioning. The slide tackle, on the other hand, is a higher-risk, higher-reward move. It's for those moments when the attacker is pulling away or you need to win the ball. Timing is everything with a slide tackle—go in too early, and you'll miss; too late, and you'll likely give up a foul or penalty. But when done correctly, there's nothing more satisfying than sweeping the ball off an attacker's feet and springing a counterattack.

- **When to use each:** You've got to read the game and the attacker. Is the player you're defending fast and looking to sprint past you? That's when a slide tackle might be your best bet. Is the attacker facing you up, trying to juke you out with footwork? A standing tackle lets you stay balanced and ready to adjust if they try to cut inside. Understanding *when* and *how* to use each tackle is key to becoming a well-rounded defender.

- **Safety and ethics:** Tackling can be risky, and it's essential to know how to tackle it fairly. You want to win the ball, not injure your opponent or risk a red card. Keep your feet low, go for the ball, and avoid coming in from behind—it's all about precision and control. Watch any top defender; you'll see how clean and ethical tackling is a crucial part of their game. You don't want to be the player known for reckless challenges—you want to be known for your skill and timing.

- **Game footage analysis:** One of the best ways to improve your tackling is by watching how the pros do it. Analyze clips of players like Virgil van Dijk or Kalidou Koulibaly—watch how they position themselves, how they time their tackles, and how they avoid overcommitting. Studying these moments can teach you a lot about how to perfect your technique.

Interception Techniques

Interceptions are all about anticipation—it's like playing chess, where you have to think two or three moves ahead. The beauty of a well-timed interception is that it stops an attack before it even begins, often turning defense into offense in the blink of an eye.

- **Anticipation and reading the play:** Intercepting a pass requires sharp instincts and an understanding of the game's flow. You've got to watch the ball and the players around you—anticipate where the pass is going before it's even made. That ability to read the play separates good defenders from great ones. A top defender doesn't just wait for the ball to come to them—they *see* the passing lanes and step in before the attacker even knows what's happening.

- **Body positioning:** Proper positioning is the foundation of successful interceptions. You want to position yourself in a way that cuts off passing lanes and forces the attacker into making a mistake. Your body should be angled so that you can spring into action, either stepping into the lane for a quick interception or closing down the attacker to pressure a poor pass. This is especially important in high-pressure moments when every second counts.

- **Simulating match scenarios:** Practice makes perfect. Drills that simulate real-game scenarios—like quick passing plays in tight spaces—are great for honing your interception skills. These drills help improve your reaction time and ability to read what's happening around you. Over time, you'll start seeing patterns in the opponent's play, making it easier to predict where the ball is going next.

Defensive Positioning

You've probably heard it a hundred times, but positioning is everything in defending. It doesn't matter how fast or strong you are—if you're out of position, you're giving attackers the advantage. The best defenders know how to position themselves to not only stop attacks but also guide play into less dangerous areas.

- **Cutting off passing lanes:** One of your main jobs as a defender is to make life difficult for the opposition. By positioning yourself correctly, you can force the attacker to make passes they don't want to make, cutting off their preferred options. You want to stay balanced, always ready to move in any direction. In training, focus on positioning drills that teach you to maintain the perfect distance—close enough to make an interception but not so close that you get beaten by a quick pass or move.

- **Balance and readiness:** Being flat-footed is a killer. You want to stay on the balls of your feet, light and ready to move at a moment's notice. This comes from drills that focus on *reactive defending*—where you practice moving side to side, backward and forward, always keeping your balance and readiness to engage or retreat.

- **Closing down without overcommitting:** Here's the tricky part—pressing an opponent without diving in too early. You want to close down the space, limit their options, and force them into a mistake, but if you overcommit, you give them a chance to get around you. It's about patience and timing. Closing down is like a dance—stay in control, keep your distance, and strike at the right moment. You'll see defenders like Sergio Ramos or Giorgio Chiellini do this brilliantly—they apply pressure without getting sucked in, waiting for the attacker to show their hand before making their move.

Team Defensive Strategies

It's great to master individual defensive skills, but soccer is a team sport, and the best defenses work as a unit. Individual brilliance is amplified when you're in sync with your teammates, moving together like a well-oiled machine.

- **Defending as a cohesive unit:** Think of the backline as a chain—when one defender moves, the others follow. You want to stay connected, moving together to close down space and eliminate passing options for the opposition. Team drills that focus on defensive shape are critical for this. Work on pressing together as a unit or dropping back in sync when the situation calls for it. The more you train these movements, the more automatic they'll become in games.

- **Press or drop?:** Knowing when to press high and drop back is key to a strong defense. If you press at the wrong moment, you're leaving gaps behind for the opponent to exploit. If you drop too early, you're giving them space to attack. Situational drills help players learn when to step up and press and when it's better to fall back and reorganize. It's all about reading the game and knowing what's needed at the moment.

- **Communication is everything:** The best defensive teams are the ones that talk constantly. You need to communicate with your teammates—warning someone to cover a player, letting them know you've got their back, or organizing the press. Clear communication between defenders and midfielders prevents breakdowns and ensures everyone knows their role in defending as a unit. If you watch teams like Manchester City or Liverpool, you'll see that their backline is constantly communicating and adjusting.

CHAPTER 4:
TEAM STRATEGIES AND FORMATIONS

Why does every soccer coach have a love-hate relationship with formations? Because, just like deciding whether to binge an extra episode or hit the gym, the right choice can make all the difference.

In this chapter, we're looking at some of the most popular soccer formations—those strategic setups that either make you look like a tactical genius or leave you wondering where it all went wrong.

From the classic 4-4-2's balanced simplicity to the aggressive, attack-first mentality of the 4-3-3, we'll break down each setup's strengths, weaknesses, and key responsibilities. So whether you're a player trying to understand your role or a fan wanting to sound smart at the next match, stick around. By the end, you'll know exactly why that 5-3-2 formation can feel like building a brick wall—or a springboard for a deadly counterattack.

4-4-2 FORMATION

They are balanced and simple. This is the go-to formation for teams who want both attack and defense without sacrificing one for the other. The two central midfielders are your engine, with wide midfielders offering support on the flanks. The forwards? They're constantly looking for opportunities, but don't forget—they help press when needed. Teams that want a solid foundation and some flexibility love this one because it keeps things structured yet allows for creativity.

Key advantage: You get width from your midfielders, stability from your defenders, and a couple of strikers who can focus on finishing. Perfect for all levels.

4-3-3 FORMATION

Attack-minded: This formation is all about pressure. You've got three forwards ready to pounce on any mistake and midfielders willing to press high up the pitch. This works well when your team has skilled wingers because they stretch the opponent's defense, opening space for your striker or central midfielders to shoot. But beware—it demands a lot of stamina and focus since your full-backs often need to join the attack.

Key advantage: When you want to dominate possession and take control of the game offensively, this one's a no-brainer.

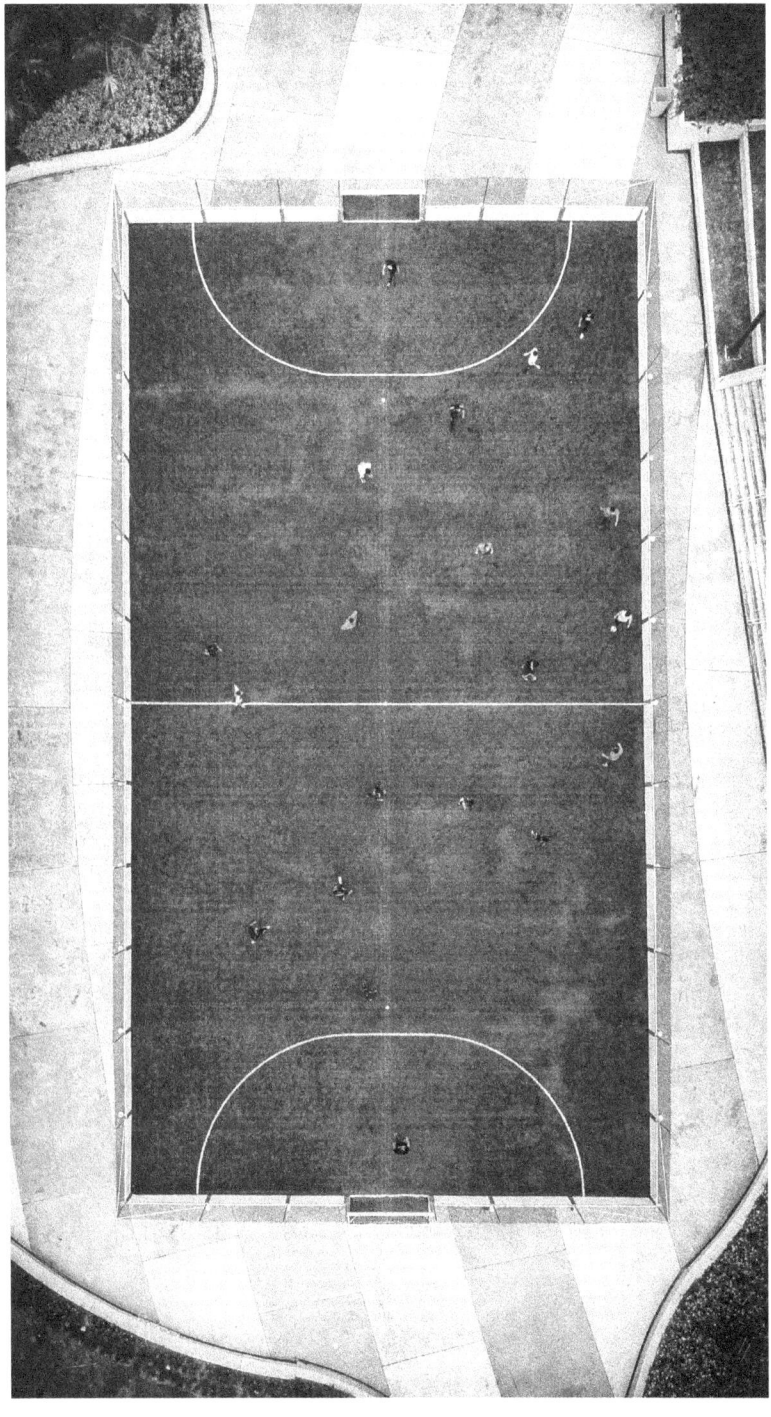

3-5-2 FORMATION

Midfield masters. Think of this as midfield heaven. Five players control the tempo, dictating where the ball goes. The wingbacks act as both defenders and attackers, constantly moving up and down the field, so they have to be incredibly fit. This is for teams that want to overwhelm the opposition in the middle but still keep defensive security.

Key advantage: Ultimate midfield control with flexibility to adapt to offense or defense as needed.

5-3-2 FORMATION

Defensive fortress. If your team wants to hunker down and counterattack, this formation sets you up perfectly. It's about having a rock-solid defense, with five at the back ready to absorb pressure. But it's not all about sitting deep; when your team wins the ball, those wingbacks can fly forward, helping launch quick counterattacks. However, transitions need to be smooth, or you'll get caught out.

Key advantage: You frustrate opponents with your defensive shape, then hit them on the break when they least expect it.

Roles and Responsibilities

Defenders: Your job? Protect the goal. In a 4-4-2, you're pressing the ball and covering spaces, ensuring you don't leave gaps for the opposition to exploit. Communication is everything—if one defender steps up, the others must shift. In a

5-3-2, you're more about holding your ground and waiting for the right moment to win back possession.

Midfielders: You're the glue. In formations like 3-5-2, you control the game. You must balance defensive duties with creating attacks, which means reading the game like a pro. Anticipate the next move and link up with the forwards seamlessly.

Forwards: You live to score. But in formations like the 4-3-3, your role includes pressing high and helping your team win the ball back. It's about creating space for your teammates, and chemistry with wingers and midfielders is crucial to breaking down the opposition's defense.

Substitutes and rotation: Even the best teams need fresh legs. Substitutes can change the game's dynamic, especially when used strategically in formations. Understanding your role, even off the bench, can make all the difference when it's time to step in.

Verbal Communication

You've got to talk on the field. Loud, clear, and constant chatter can make or break a team's rhythm. Calling out plays, shouting "man on" when an opponent is closing in, or just giving a quick "good job" can lift your team's energy. Effective communication builds a vibe, which affects how your team performs under pressure. Think about pros—Cristiano Ronaldo doesn't just score goals; he commands the game with his voice.

Examples of Key Phrases
- "Switch it!" for shifting play to the opposite side.
- "Drop back!" when a defender needs to retreat.
- "Time!" when a teammate has space to control the ball.

Non-Verbal Communication

Not everything on the pitch needs words. Sometimes, the most powerful communication is silent. Ever notice how a glance between defenders can mean "I've got your back" or how wingers use hand signals to show where they want the ball? Non-verbal cues, like a simple point or eye contact, can cut through the chaos when yelling isn't an option.

Practice tip: Try drills where your team has to play silently, relying only on body language and eye contact to coordinate. It's harder than it sounds, but you'll see how much better you get at reading each other.

Communication in Transitions

This is where games are often won or lost—those rapid switches between attack and defense. In these moments, quick, decisive communication is everything. When you lose possession, the first thing you need to hear is "Get back!" or "Cover left!" When you win it, it's "Push up!" or "Spread out!" It's not about shouting aimlessly; each call should direct your team and snap them into action.

Stay alert: Always be the player talking during those transitional moments. The quicker your team can react, the better the outcome.

Creating a Positive Communication Environment

Nobody likes a teammate who only yells criticisms. Building a culture of constructive communication means players are more likely to listen and respond well. Team meetings are a good place to hash out how you communicate on the field, and ensuring everyone feels heard fosters respect.

Pro tip: Always balance feedback with encouragement. You want a team that can lift each other, especially when the pressure mounts.

Analyzing Opponent Strengths and Weaknesses

Scouting an opponent isn't just for coaches. You can do it too. Watch their games, know their key players, and spot their weak points. If the opposing full-back loves to bomb forward, you know to exploit that space behind them. If their striker is fast but not great in the air, get tight to them and force them to play long balls.

Research tip: Before the game, watch videos or look for match reports. Understand how they are set up and where they might be vulnerable.

Flexible Formation Adjustments

One thing you'll notice with elite teams is their ability to switch formations on the fly. If your team starts in a 4-4-2, but the opponents are flooding the midfield, maybe it's time to switch to a 4-3-3 or drop into a 5-3-2 to clog up space. The best players don't just stick to one plan—they adapt based on what's happening on the pitch.

Game-changing moment: Imagine your team is struggling to get out of your half. By switching to a more defensive formation, you could relieve pressure, regroup, and launch a counter-attack.

Responding to Game Progression

Soccer isn't static—it's constantly changing. So should your tactics. Maybe their star player has an off day—time to press higher and take advantage. Or maybe your defense is struggling with their wingers—time to pull back and absorb pressure. Either way, you've got to keep thinking, keep watching, and keep talking.

Leadership role: Every team needs someone to recognize when it's time to adapt. Be that player—whether suggesting a shift in formation or simply telling your teammates to drop deeper.

Learning From Matches

After each game, review what worked and what didn't. Discuss with your team how you adapted (or didn't) and what you could have done better. This kind of analysis will make you a smarter player, and smarter players will win more games.

Pro tip: Keep a journal of key moments from your matches. Write down how your team adapted and what the outcome was so next time, you're better prepared.

CHAPTER 5:
THE MENTAL GAME

Ever try focusing on a task, and suddenly, you're thinking about what to eat after practice? Concentration and focus are the unsung heroes of soccer—right up there with fancy footwork and highlight-reel goals. You can be the fastest, strongest, or most technically gifted player on the field, but if you're zoning out at key moments, all that potential goes to waste.

Take Lionel Messi, for example. His genius isn't just in his dribbling—it's his ability to stay locked in while 22 players and a roaring crowd go wild around him. The mental sharpness players like Messi and Kevin De Bruyne display doesn't happen by chance; it's developed. It helps them consistently pull off magic under pressure while lesser players crumble.

In this chapter, we'll be talking about strategies that will help you build focus and make it your competitive edge. You'll learn to train your brain to keep you sharp from kickoff to final whistle, even when the game's on the line.

DEVELOPING CONCENTRATION AND FOCUS

Being a great soccer player isn't just about flashy footwork or powerful shots—it's about having the mental edge that keeps you sharp and ready for anything. Think about players like Lionel Messi or Kevin De Bruyne. They don't just rely on their skills; they dominate because they can maintain laser focus in the heat of the game, no matter what chaos is happening around them.

Let's break down how you can build that concentration level and make it your secret weapon.

The Importance of Focus

Why is focus so essential? Because a split-second of inattention can cost you the game. Imagine you're in the final minutes of a tied match and miss a critical pass because your mind drifted. Now, think of players like Sergio Ramos, whose ability to stay focused often results in last-minute game-saving plays. Focus helps you:

- **React quickly** to changes in the field.
- **Execute strategies** and skills without hesitation.
- **Avoid mistakes** that could let your team down.

When locked in, you make better decisions, faster movements, and smarter plays—key ingredients to becoming the best.

Techniques to Improve Focus

1. Mindfulness exercises

Ever wonder how top athletes stay cool under pressure? Mindfulness helps them stay present and block out distractions. Before practice or a game, try focusing on your breathing for a few minutes. It's a simple trick to calm your mind and keep it in the moment.

2. **Short-duration focus drills**

Think of concentration as a muscle—you have to train it. Start small, like spending 5-10 minutes during practice solely concentrating on one thing (e.g., keeping possession). Build up from there, like a sprinter trains to run longer distances. Soon, you'll notice you can stay focused longer, even during grueling matches.

3. **Visualization**

Cristiano Ronaldo is famous for using visualization to prepare for big moments. Before your next match, close your eyes and picture yourself making key plays— winning tackles, perfectly placed passes, or a game-winning shot. This mental rehearsal sharpens your focus when the real thing comes.

Creating a Focus-Friendly Environment

1. **Pre-game rituals**

Top athletes have pre-game routines to get in the zone. Maybe it's listening to a certain song, repeating a mantra, or doing a specific warm-up. Find what calms you and builds focus so that by the time you're on the field, you're fully dialed in.

2. **Minimize distractions**

Whether you're at practice or playing in a game, distractions can kill your focus. It's like trying to listen to your coach while your teammates joke around— you'll miss the critical stuff. Train yourself to tune out distractions, whether crowd noise or on-field drama, so you stay locked in.

3. **Set focus goals**

   Give yourself one focus target for each practice or game. For example, "I'm going to focus on perfecting my passing" or "I'll concentrate on tracking my opponent closely." It gives you a specific, bite-sized challenge to work on, making your training more purposeful.

Tracking Progress

1. **Keep a focus journal**

   Just like keeping track of your fitness progress, writing down notes about your focus levels can help. After each practice or game, describe how well you stayed concentrated and what distracted you. Over time, you'll spot patterns and find ways to improve.

2. **Get feedback**

   Your coach or teammates might notice things you don't. Ask them how they think you're doing in terms of focus. Maybe you're zoning out during crucial plays or losing attention at the end of a match—feedback can help you fix these blind spots.

3. **Adjust your routine**

   As you track your progress, tweak your training routine to include more focus-enhancing drills. If visualization works for you, keep it up. If you're easily distracted, find strategies to minimize those disruptions. The goal is a steady improvement, game by game.

By building your focus, you're setting yourself up as a game-changer on the field. Concentration isn't just a skill; it's a competitive edge that can elevate your entire performance. Keep practicing, stay mindful, and watch your game soar.

OVERCOMING PERFORMANCE ANXIETY: PLAY LIKE THE PROS EVEN UNDER PRESSURE

Ever feel that pit in your stomach right before a big match? Or maybe your legs feel like lead, and your mind is racing with all the ways things could go wrong? Well, guess what? You're not alone. Even legends like Neymar and Harry Kane have been there—they just learned how to deal with it.

This section is all about turning that performance anxiety into something you can manage so that when the pressure's on, you can still crush it.

Understanding Anxiety's Impact

First off, let's talk about how anxiety can affect your game. Ever notice how when you're nervous, your passes might be off, or you start second-guessing yourself? That's anxiety messing with your confidence. Players like Kylian Mbappé have discussed the pressure to perform in big matches and how it can lead to mistakes if not handled right.

But here's the kicker: everyone experiences it. The key is to recognize when it's happening and why. Maybe it's the crowd or the fear of making a mistake—whatever your triggers are, knowing them is the first step in getting control.

Coping Strategies for Anxiety

1. **Breathing exercises**

   When anxiety hits, your body gets tense, and your breathing can go haywire. That's why staying in control of your breath is a game-changer. Before kickoff, try a simple breathing exercise: inhale for 4 seconds, hold for 4, and exhale for 4. Repeat it a few times, and you'll feel more grounded, calm, and ready to take on the field.

2. **Pre-game routine**

   Take a page from Cristiano Ronaldo's book—he has a pre-game routine that helps him feel in control, no matter the stakes. Whether it's listening to a playlist, stretching in a specific order, or doing a certain warm-up, routines can help make the unfamiliar feel familiar. And that comfort? It's anxiety's worst enemy.

3. Positive self-talk

When you're nervous, your brain can spiral into negative thinking—stuff like, "What if I miss that shot?" or "What if I mess up?" Flip the script with positive self-talk. Repeat mantras like "I've trained for this" or "I'm ready." Zlatan Ibrahimović is known for his confidence; a big part of that comes from controlling the narrative in his head. If you believe you can do it, you're already halfway there.

Visualizing Success

1. Imagining victory

Think about Megan Rapinoe standing at the penalty spot. She doesn't imagine missing—she imagines herself hitting the perfect shot. Visualization is a powerful tool to calm your nerves. Close your eyes and see yourself pulling off that perfect pass or nailing the game-winning goal. The more vividly you picture it, the more real it becomes.

2. Rehearse game scenarios

Picture yourself in tricky game situations. How do you handle it? Visualize the pass, the run, the tackle. By mentally rehearsing these moments, you're tricking your brain into feeling like you've been there before. It's like taking the unknown out of the equation and, with it, much of the anxiety.

Seeking Support

1. **Talk to someone**

   You don't have to go through it alone. Share what you're feeling with a coach or teammate—they've been there too. Famous players like Marcus Rashford have been open about struggling with performance anxiety and how talking to others has helped them cope. Whether it's pre-game nerves or a rough patch, communication can lead to support and practical advice.

2. **Mental health resources**

   Sometimes anxiety goes deeper than just game-day jitters, and that's okay. Seeking out mental health professionals, like a sports psychologist, can give you tools and techniques specific to your needs. Players like Michael Phelps have credited therapy for helping them manage pressure and anxiety throughout their careers.

3. **Supportive coaches and teams**

   It's crucial to be in an environment where you can express your feelings without fear. Coaches who create a safe space for players to talk about mental health not only help individuals but build stronger, more connected teams.

Anxiety is something every player deals with, from rookies to superstars. The difference is in how you handle it. By using strategies like breathing exercises, visualization, and opening up about your struggles, you can keep stress from taking over. The more you practice managing your anxiety, the more confident and resilient you'll become—both on and off the field.

Goal Setting and Motivation

You want to become the best soccer player, right? Let's start with something crucial: setting goals that get you there. Goals are like your game plan—they tell you where you're going and how to get there. Let's break it down, starting with the SMART Goals Framework.

1. **Specific goals**

   Don't just say, "I want to improve at soccer." What part of your game? Dribbling like Messi? Defending like Van Dijk? Be specific so you know exactly what you're aiming for. When Kylian Mbappé decided he wanted to be one of the fastest forwards, he didn't just run aimlessly—he focused on improving his speed and control.

2. **Measurable goals**

   If you want to score more goals, set a number: "I'll score 10 goals this season." Measuring progress is key. Cristiano Ronaldo doesn't just say, "I want to be better"—he sets records and tracks them!

3. **Achievable goals**

   Goals must push you, but don't aim for something way out of reach. Can you dribble through an entire team right now? Maybe not, but could you improve your 1v1 skills by next month? Absolutely. Step by step, just like Kevin De Bruyne did—he mastered one skill at a time.

4. **Relevant goals**

   Your personal goals should align with your team's objectives. If you're playing as a midfielder, you need goals that help the team's flow, like improving your passing accuracy or game awareness, rather than focusing on scoring.

5. **Time-bound goals**

Set a deadline. If you want to improve your weak foot by the end of the season, make it happen in a set time frame. Deadlines bring urgency. Neymar didn't become a star overnight, but he had clear timeframes for improvement during his early years at Santos.

Now, let's talk about keeping that motivation alive. Big goals can be overwhelming, so break them down into smaller, manageable tasks. Are they scoring more? Start with aiming for one goal in the next game and build from there.

Find your intrinsic motivation—the love of the game. Why do you play? Maybe you love the rush of a perfect pass or the feeling of victory. Tap into that. And when you hit milestones, celebrate—scored with your weak foot for the first time? That's huge—acknowledge it.

Accountability is essential. Keep a journal to note your progress, thoughts, and areas to improve. Pair up with a teammate or coach to keep each other on track. Reflection is your secret weapon—look back on how far you've come and adjust where necessary.

Lastly, create a long-term vision. Imagine where you want to be in five or ten years. Maybe you see yourself playing for a top club or leading your school team to victory. Make a vision board of your soccer heroes and future dreams. Visualize it, and connect every training session to that future.

Visualization Techniques

If you want to level up your game, it's time to master a tool all the pros use: visualization. It's more than just daydreaming— training your mind to be ready before your body even moves.

1. **What is visualization?**

     Think of it as a mental rehearsal. You're sitting quietly, but in your mind, you're already on the field, dribbling past defenders, nailing that perfect pass, or saving a penalty. This mental practice builds muscle memory and helps you perform under pressure. Take LeBron James—he's known for using visualization to calm nerves and prep for big moments, and it works in soccer, too. By visualizing yourself in-game situations, you become familiar with the pressure, reducing anxiety when the whistle blows.

2. **Techniques for effective visualization**

     Start by creating a detailed mental image of a successful moment. Let's say you're practicing penalty kicks. Picture yourself stepping up, focusing on the ball, hearing the crowd, feeling the tension in the air, and then placing the ball perfectly in the corner of the net. Involve all your senses—the smell of the grass, the roar of the crowd, the weight of the ball at your feet. It makes the imagery vivid and impactful.

Build a routine. Spend a few minutes before every practice or game in visualization mode. Make it a habit; soon, it'll feel as natural as lacing up your cleats.

1. **Integrating visualization with training**

   Don't just visualize and leave it there. Combine it with physical training. Before a drill, take a moment to imagine yourself completing it perfectly and then execute it. After a game, replay key moments in your head—what worked, what didn't, and how you can improve. This mental review strengthens your strategic thinking and makes you sharper for the next match.

2. **Success stories**

   Plenty of top players swear by visualization. Brazilian legend Pelé often spoke about how he would visualize his matches ahead of time, imagining himself dribbling, passing, and scoring. It was like playing the game twice— once in his head and once on the field. More recently, Liverpool's Virgil van Dijk talked about how visualization helped him maintain his cool and consistency under pressure.

You can try it too. Whether preparing for a match or recovering from a loss, take time to visualize and watch how it sharpens your skills.

CHAPTER 6:
FITNESS AND CONDITIONING

You know that feeling when you're halfway through a soccer match, and your legs start questioning every life choice you've ever made? Yeah, that's your body begging for more endurance training. If you want to be the player still sprinting in the 90th minute while everyone else is gasping for air, this chapter is for you.

Building stamina isn't just about running aimlessly around the pitch until you collapse. It's about training smart, not just hard. From boosting your cardiovascular endurance to ensuring your legs have enough juice to outlast your opponents, we're about to break down everything you need to turn yourself into a 90-minute machine.

ENDURANCE TRAINING FOR SOCCER PLAYERS

Want to keep running like a machine for the full 90 minutes? Building endurance is key; in soccer, stamina is your best friend. Let's get into how to develop it effectively.

1. Aerobic conditioning

Endurance starts with your heart and lungs. If you're gasping for air after ten minutes, how can you chase down that breakaway in the 80th minute? That's where aerobic exercises like long-distance running come in. Running steadily for extended periods improves your cardiovascular endurance, meaning you'll have the energy to keep going, even when the match is pushing into extra time.

Not into long, boring runs? Mix it up with interval training. Alternate between jogging and sprinting. For example, sprint for 30 seconds, then jog for a minute and repeat. It's how elite players like Mo Salah build the stamina to sprint up and down the wing for 90 minutes. Add these sessions a couple of times a week, and you'll see improvement in both your stamina and recovery.

2. Interval runs

Soccer isn't about running at a steady pace—it's all about quick bursts and sudden stops. That's why interval runs are a game-changer. By alternating between high-intensity sprints and slower recovery jogs, you're mimicking the exact type of movement you do during a match.

Imagine you're trying to keep up with a fast winger—you sprint to cut them off, then slow down as the play develops, only to sprint again moments later. High-intensity interval training (HIIT) helps you build the ability to recover faster, meaning you'll be fresh for the next sprint when it counts most. Try drills like 40-yard sprints, followed by a slow jog back to the start, and repeat.

3. **Sustained speed**

   It's not just about sprinting fast—it's about doing it repeatedly, even in the last minutes of the game. To maintain sustained speed, you need endurance to recover quickly after each sprint. Players like Kylian Mbappé train specifically to sprint at top speed multiple times per match.

To train for this, try tempo runs—run at 70-80% of your top speed for longer distances (400 meters), then rest and repeat. Over time, your body will get used to sustaining higher speeds for longer.

4. **Monitoring progress**

   Tracking your progress isn't just for school—it's essential for seeing how far you've come. Start a training log, where you note the distances you run and the time it takes. Wearable devices or apps can track your fitness levels, showing you how much ground you cover in a match or how fast your sprint times are improving.

When you see progress, it motivates you to keep pushing through those tough conditioning sessions. If you hit a plateau, mix things up with new drills or increase the intensity of your workouts to push yourself past it.

STRENGTH AND CONDITIONING EXERCISES

Building endurance is just one part of the equation—you also need the strength to push past opponents, jump higher for headers, and shoot with more power. Let's break down how to get stronger and smarter.

1. Core strength

A solid core is the foundation of every great soccer player. It helps you balance when dribbling, hold your position when shielding the ball, and unleash powerful shots. Players like Cristiano Ronaldo don't just rely on leg power for their famous free kicks—their core muscles do a lot of the work.

For a stronger core, try exercises like **planks**, **Russian twists**, and **medicine ball throws**. They'll help you stabilize your body in challenging situations, whether twisting past a defender or launching a long-range pass. A strong core helps prevent injuries, especially in your back and hips.

2. Leg strength

Your legs do the heavy lifting in soccer—literally. To improve your speed, agility, and ability to out-jump opponents, focus on **leg-specific exercises**. Players like Erling Haaland use squats, lunges, and **leg presses** to build the explosive power that makes them deadly in front of the goal.

Start with bodyweight exercises, then gradually add weights as you build strength. Focus on power and control—strong legs make you faster, more agile, and less likely to get injured.

3. Upper body conditioning

Soccer isn't just about leg work. A strong upper body can give you an edge in tackles, help you shield the ball more effectively, and improve your overall physicality on the field. Think of Zlatan Ibrahimović—he's got the strength to hold off defenders and control the ball with ease.

Add exercises like **push-ups**, **rows**, and **pull-ups** into your routine to build arm, shoulder, and back strength. But remember, you're not trying to bulk up like a bodybuilder— you're building strength that translates to better balance, agility, and resilience on the field.

4. Functional movements

Strength training should always complement your game. That's why it's important to incorporate **functional movements**—exercises that mimic real soccer actions, like twisting, cutting, and changing direction. **Lateral lunges** and **single-leg deadlifts** can help you build strength in ways that directly translate to your performance on the pitch.

Create a workout plan that works alongside your soccer training. That way, you're not just getting stronger—you're getting **stronger for soccer**.

Endurance and strength training are the backbone of elite soccer performance. Whether chasing down attackers in the final minutes or blasting shots from outside the box, your fitness will set you apart. By incorporating aerobic conditioning, interval training, and strength exercises into your routine, you'll become faster, stronger, and more resilient, ready to dominate every minute of every game.

Flexibility and Injury Prevention: Stay Agile, Stay Healthy

If you want to play soccer at your best, flexibility isn't just a bonus—it's a must-have superpower! It keeps you nimble on the field and, most importantly, prevents injuries that can sideline you. Let's dive into key routines that should be part of your game.

Dynamic Stretching

Before the game or a tough practice session, dynamic stretching is your secret weapon. It gets your muscles fired up and ready for action. Think about your favorite players, like Lionel Messi or Megan Rapinoe—you'll catch them warming up with leg swings or arm circles. These exercises wake up the muscles needed to fly across the field. Try a routine like this:

- **Leg swings:** Forward and sideways, loosening your hips and hamstrings.
- **Arm circles:** Get your shoulders in gear. Incorporate these movements into your warm-ups; you'll feel more explosive from the get-go. It's a simple, fast routine that makes a difference.

Static stretching: Cooling down like a champion: When the game's over or practice winds down, it's all about the cool down. Post-activity static stretching helps your muscles recover, stay flexible, and reduce soreness. Players like Cristiano Ronaldo are known for their meticulous post-match routines, including stretches targeting key muscle groups. Focus on areas like:

- **Quads and hamstrings:** Standing quad stretches and hamstring reach-outs.
- **Calves:** A deep calf stretch can save you from cramping up later. Commit to a post-game stretch every time; over time, you'll notice increased flexibility and fewer injuries.

Balance and coordination: The foundation of every move: Balance is crucial in soccer, whether fending off an opponent or landing a header. To sharpen this skill, activities like yoga or using a balance board can train your body to stay steady. Top pros like Zlatan Ibrahimović swear by balance training for better footwork and injury prevention. Exercises like one-legged stands or yoga poses such as the tree pose might seem simple, but they're effective in keeping you nimble during those sharp turns or quick pivots on the field.

Listen to your body: Don't play the hero: The golden rule? Know when to back off. Soccer legends who have played for years have mastered the art of listening to their bodies. Feeling a twinge in your knee? Don't ignore it. Adjust your training—cut back when necessary—and prioritize rest and recovery. This smart approach keeps top players in the game for the long haul. Remember, rest days are just as important as training days!

SOCCER-SPECIFIC AGILITY DRILLS

Soccer agility drills aren't just drills—they're the magic tricks that separate good players from the great ones. They make you faster, sharper, and practically untouchable. Here's how to take your agility to the next level.

Ladder Drills: Speed at your feet: The agility ladder isn't just some fancy piece of equipment—it's your fast track to better footwork. When you practice drills like **high knees** or **side shuffles**, you train your body to move quickly and precisely, like a top-tier striker who evades defenders with lightning-fast feet. Get a ladder and start small, focusing on clean, quick steps. Over time, you'll notice the difference on the field—your feet will feel like they're moving at double speed.

Cone Drills: Change direction like a pro: Cone drills sharpen your ability to cut and turn, which is crucial for beating opponents. Picture yourself in a one-on-one with a defender—

cone drills help you change direction so quickly they won't know what hit them. Try **T-drills** or **zig-zags**, where you sprint forward, shuffle sideways, and backpedal around cones. Adjust the cone distance to ramp up the challenge. This skill is key to staying ahead during those intense midfield scrambles or sprints down the sideline.

Plyometric exercises: Explosive power: Want to be faster off the line? Plyometric exercises like **box jump** and **burpees** build explosive strength in your legs, which helps with sprints and headers. Remember, it's all about power in short bursts. And pros know this—Gareth Bale's jaw-dropping speed is partly thanks to his ploy training. Just follow safety tips—focus on landing softly to avoid injury and build up gradually.

Reaction time drills: Think fast, move faster: Soccer's not just about how fast you can run—it's how quickly you can react. Set up reaction time drills that mimic game situations: shout "Go!" and have a friend or coach throw the ball in different directions. Your job is to react and sprint toward it as fast as possible. A faster reaction time could be between intercepting a crucial pass or missing a game-saving tackle.

CHAPTER 7:
NUTRITION FOR PEAK PERFORMANCE

Think of your body like a high-performance machine; just like any top athlete, what you put into that machine is crucial to how well it performs. Whether you're sprinting down the soccer field, making a last-minute tackle, or recovering after a tough match, the right fuel—your diet—plays a massive role in your success.

But it's not just about eating more or loading up on energy drinks; it's about balance, timing, and knowing exactly what your body needs. In this chapter, we're going to break down the fundamentals of nutrition for soccer players. You'll learn about:

- **Macronutrients:** Carbohydrates, proteins, and fats—the three essential fuel types that power your game, help your muscles recover and keep you performing at your best.
- **Micronutrients:** Vitamins and minerals may seem like the background players, but they're critical for keeping you injury-free and ready to compete.
- **Meal timing:** When you eat is just as important as what you eat. We'll cover how to fuel up before practice

and games and how to recover afterward with the right nutrition.

- **Hydration:** Water is more than just a thirst-quencher—it's the key to avoiding fatigue, cramps, and injuries, so we'll dive into the importance of staying properly hydrated on and off the field.

- **Supplements:** Do you really need them? We'll explore the pros and cons of using supplements to enhance your game.

By the end of this guide, you'll have a clearer understanding of how to fuel your body correctly—both on game day and in everyday life. Whether you're chasing that extra burst of speed or recovering after a tough match, this is the blueprint for fueling your best performance.

BALANCED DIET ESSENTIALS FOR YOUNG ATHLETES

You wouldn't put the wrong fuel in a race car, right? The same goes for your body, especially when you're out there giving it your all on the soccer field; what you eat matters—big time. Let's break down what a solid diet for soccer players looks like and how it'll help you perform at your peak.

Macronutrients

Every soccer player needs to understand the big three: carbohydrates, proteins, and fats. They're the fuel that keeps you going and helps your body recover from all the running, tackling, and sprinting.

- **Carbohydrates** are your main energy source. Think of carbs like the gas that powers a car. When you're training hard or playing in a match, your body uses up energy fast, and carbs (like whole grains, fruits, and vegetables) keep your energy tank full. Ever wonder why pro players have pasta the night before a game? That's why.

- **Proteins** are your recovery squad. After an intense match or practice, your muscles need to repair and grow stronger, and that's where protein comes in. Foods like chicken, fish, eggs, and beans are packed with the protein your body craves to rebuild muscle. For young athletes like you, who are still growing, this is even more important.

- **Fats** aren't the bad guys here. They're like the backup energy source your body can tap into when needed. Healthy fats—like those from avocados, nuts, and olive oil—also keep your body functioning properly, helping with everything from brain function to joint health. Players like Cristiano Ronaldo include healthy fats in their diet to maintain peak physical shape.

Micronutrients:
The Little Things That Make a Big Difference

While macronutrients are your main fuel, micronutrients—vitamins and minerals—keep your engine running smoothly. Missing out on these can hurt your performance, even if you don't feel it immediately.

- **Vitamin D** is crucial for bone health. If you're running up and down the field for 90 minutes, you need strong bones to avoid injuries. Get enough sunlight (hello, outdoor training!) or include foods like fish and fortified cereals in your diet.

- **Iron** helps your blood carry oxygen to your muscles, which keeps you going during long training sessions. If you're feeling tired all the time, you might be low on iron. Foods like spinach, red meat, and beans can help with that.

- **Calcium** is a must for bone strength, especially for young athletes who are still growing. You'll find it in dairy products like milk, cheese, and yogurt, which help prevent stress fractures and other bone injuries.

Meal Timing: Eating Like a Pro

Eating the right food is important, but *when* you eat, it can make or break your performance.

- **Pre-training meals** should be light and packed with energy. A small meal or snack with carbs and a little protein about 1–2 hours before you hit the field works best. Try something like whole grain toast with peanut butter or a banana with yogurt to fuel up.
- **Post-game meals** are all about recovery. After a tough match or practice, your muscles are tired and need fuel to rebuild. Aim for a meal within an hour that has protein and carbs—like a chicken with rice or a smoothie with protein powder, milk, and fruit.

Healthy Snack Options: Power up on the Go

Soccer players are always on the move, so having easy, healthy snacks on hand is a game-changer. Here are some simple, nutritious snacks that won't slow you down:

- **Fruit:** Bananas, apples, and oranges are packed with quick energy.
- **Yogurt:** A protein-packed option that's easy to grab.
- **Nuts:** Almonds or mixed nuts offer healthy fats and a protein boost. These snacks are easy to carry in your bag and keep your energy up between meals or during long training sessions.

Key takeaway: Eating right isn't just about filling your stomach—it's about fueling your performance. By understanding how to balance carbs, proteins, and fats, keeping up with key vitamins and minerals, and timing your meals properly, you'll feel stronger, last longer, and recover faster. Fuel your body correctly, and the field is yours to dominate.

Hydration and Its Importance:
Fuel Your Game With Water

Hydration is your secret weapon on the soccer field—keeping you sharp, strong, and ready to dominate. Whether in the middle of a match or just training, staying hydrated is essential for peak performance. Let's break it down.

Understanding Hydration Needs: Fuel for Your Body

Hydration isn't just about drinking water when you're thirsty. It's about ensuring your body has enough fluid to keep going strong, even during intense training or games. When you sweat, you lose water, and if you don't replace it, your performance suffers—big time. Fatigue, cramping, and slower reactions are just a few of the consequences.

Here's how to stay ahead:

- **Before a game:** Start hydrating hours before. Aim to drink about 16-20 ounces of water 2-3 hours before kick-off. You should be sipping regularly, not chugging all at once.

- **During a match or training:** Take 5-10 ounces every 20 minutes, especially during half-time. If you're feeling sluggish or cramping, it's probably time to grab some water.

- **After the game:** You've worked hard—now it's time to replace what you've lost. Within 30 minutes, drink 16-24 ounces of water, and if you've been sweating a lot, an electrolyte drink can help replenish minerals.

A quick way to check if you're hydrated? **Your urine should be pale yellow**—a darker color means you need more water.

Signs of Dehydration:
Know When You're Running on Empty

Dehydration is the enemy of every soccer player, and it creeps up fast. If you're not getting enough water, your body will start sending warning signals. Look out for:

- **Dizziness or lightheadedness:** This is your brain's way of telling you it's not getting enough blood flow.
- **Fatigue:** If you feel like you're dragging on the field, dehydration could be the reason.
- **Muscle cramps:** When your muscles don't have enough fluid, they can seize up mid-game. Ouch.

Chronic dehydration can have long-term effects, too, like making you more prone to injuries or slowing your recovery. So, don't wait until you feel thirsty to hydrate—your body is already low on fluids by then.

Electrolytes and Recovery: More Than Just Water

When you sweat, you lose electrolytes—minerals like sodium, potassium, and magnesium that help your body maintain fluid balance and muscle function. If you've ever had a cramp mid-game, that's probably due to low electrolytes.

This is where **sports drinks** or **electrolyte supplements** come in. They're not just flavored water—they replace the electrolytes you've lost, especially during longer or high-intensity matches. After a hard game, a drink with electrolytes can help speed up your recovery, so you're back at full strength faster.

Hydration Strategies: Stay On Top of It

Drinking water during practice isn't enough. Hydration is an all-day commitment. Here's how to stay hydrated around the clock:

- **Start your day with water:** As soon as you wake up, have a glass of water. It kickstarts your hydration for the day.
- **Carry a water bottle:** Make it a habit to sip water throughout the day, even when you're not training. Keep it handy during school, while studying, or just hanging out.
- **Hydrate around training:** Drink 16 ounces of water about an hour before practice and continue sipping during breaks.

Pro players know that proper hydration can make the difference between winning and losing. Just ask stars like Kylian Mbappé or Alex Morgan—they treat water like a performance-enhancing tool.

Key Takeaway: Hydration is the foundation of your athletic performance. By staying on top of your water intake, recognizing signs of dehydration, and replenishing electrolytes after tough games, you'll keep your body in peak condition, ready to own the field.

Pre-Game and Post-Game Nutrition Tips: Fuel Up, Recover Strong

Regarding soccer, nutrition isn't just about staying healthy—it's about giving your body the right fuel to perform at its best and recover quickly. Whether you're gearing up for a big match or bouncing back afterward, what you eat matters as much as your training. Let's dig into the details.

Pre-Game Nutrition: Fuel for the Fight

Before a game, your body needs fuel to power you through the full 90 minutes (and extra time, if it comes to that!). The key here is focusing on foods that provide **long-lasting energy** and prevent you from feeling sluggish or cramping up mid-game.

- **Carbohydrates** are your go-to energy source. Think of them like the gas in your car's tank. Aim for easily digestible carbs like whole grain toast, oatmeal, or brown rice. Something light and carb-heavy 1-3 hours before the game will help keep your energy high.

- **Proteins** are your body's defense team. They protect your muscles from breaking down during a hard game. Choose lean protein sources like grilled chicken or yogurt to fuel muscles without feeling too heavy.

- **Avoid heavy fats and too much fiber** before a match—things like greasy burgers or lots of beans can sit in your stomach and cause discomfort when running around the field. Stick to easily digestible meals that won't weigh you down.

Sample Pre-Game Meal (3 hours before the game)

- Grilled chicken with quinoa and steamed veggies
- A banana and a handful of almonds for extra carbs and protein

Sample Pre-Game Snack (1 hour before the game)

- A **p**iece of toast with peanut butter and a small handful of berries
- A low-fat yogurt with some honey drizzled on top

Timing Your Meals: When to Eat

Timing your pre-game meal is just as important as what you eat. Eating too late can make you feel sluggish while eating too early might leave you hungry by halftime. Here's how to time it right:

- **2-3 hours before:** A full meal with carbs, protein, and some fats is ideal. This gives your body time to digest and turn that food into energy.
- **1 hour before:** If you're closer to game time, go for a lighter snack that's easy to digest but still packed with energy. A banana or a slice of toast with peanut butter works great.

Keep in mind that everyone's body is different. Some players might feel great eating 30 minutes before the game, while others need more time—experiment during practice to see what works best for you.

Post-Game Recovery: Rebuild and Recharge

After you've left it all on the field, your body is in recovery mode. The goal now is to **replenish lost nutrients** and help your muscles recover quickly so you're ready for the next game.

- **Proteins** are key for muscle repair. Your muscles have been working hard, and they need protein to rebuild stronger. Think of foods like grilled chicken, fish, or a protein shake.
- **Carbohydrates** are also essential post-game because they refill your energy stores. After a match, your body's energy reserves are depleted, so foods like rice, pasta, or even a recovery drink with a mix of carbs and protein will help get you back to full strength.
- **Fluids and electrolytes:** You've lost a lot of fluids through sweat, so rehydration is crucial. Water is great, but if it's been a long, intense game, something with electrolytes (like a sports drink) can help balance out what your body has lost.

Sample Post-Game Recovery Meal (within 1 hour)

- Grilled salmon with sweet potatoes and steamed broccoli
- A fruit smoothie with protein powder, almond milk, and spinach

Sample Post-Game Snack

- A turkey sandwich on whole-grain bread with a slice of cheese
- A handful of trail mix with nuts and dried fruit

Tracking Your Nutrition:
Find What Works Best for You

Every player is different, and your nutrition needs might vary based on your position, playing style, and even how your body reacts to different foods. **Keep a food log** to track your feelings after eating certain meals or snacks. Did that pre-game pasta give you a boost of energy or make you feel sluggish? Did you recover faster with a certain post-game meal?

A **food diary** can help you fine-tune your nutrition so you're always at your best. Write down what you eat, when, and how you feel during training or games. Over time, you'll see patterns and learn what fuels you best.

Key Takeaway

Your pre- and post-game nutrition are as important as your skills on the field. Eating the right foods at the right times will help you fuel up, perform better, and recover faster. With a bit of experimenting and tracking, you'll find the perfect game-day nutrition plan that works for you.

Supplements:
Pros and Cons—What You Need to Know

As young athletes, you're always looking for ways to boost your performance on the soccer field. While a balanced diet is the foundation of your nutrition, many players consider supplements a quick fix to enhance their game. But before you dive into the supplement world, let's break down the pros and cons so you can make informed decisions that benefit your health and performance.

Common Supplements for Athletes: What's Out There?

When it comes to supplements, you'll find a whole array of options. Here are a few of the most common:

- **Protein powders:** These can help with muscle recovery and growth, especially if you struggle to get enough protein from whole foods. Whey protein is popular, but plant-based options are also available for those who prefer them.
- **Vitamins and minerals:** Essential for overall health, these might be necessary if your diet lacks certain nutrients. For example, vitamin D and calcium are crucial for bone health, while iron supports oxygen transport in the blood, which is important for endurance.
- **Energy gels and bars:** These can be convenient for quick energy during games or long training sessions. They're packed with carbohydrates and can help keep your energy levels up when needed.

While these supplements can be helpful, remember they're called "supplements" for a reason—they should complement your diet, not replace it!

Understanding the Need: Do You Need Supplements?

Before reaching for that protein powder or energy gel, ask yourself if supplements are necessary. Here are some criteria to consider:

- **Dietary intake:** Are you getting enough nutrients from your food? If you're eating a balanced diet rich in fruits, vegetables, whole grains, and lean proteins, you may not need supplements at all. Whole foods provide a synergistic effect—meaning the nutrients work together in ways that supplements often can't replicate.

- **Specific scenarios:** There are situations where supplements might be beneficial. For example, if you're a vegetarian or vegan, you might need extra Vitamin B12, iron, or omega-3 fatty acids typically found in animal products. If you have specific dietary restrictions or health conditions, it's worth discussing with a healthcare provider.

Always remember: the best way to fuel your body is through a well-rounded diet. Supplements can help fill gaps, but they're not a substitute for real food.

Potential Risks and Side Effects: Be Aware!

While supplements can be beneficial, they're not without risks. Here are some potential downsides to be aware of:

- **Digestive issues:** Some supplements can cause stomach upset, bloating, or other digestive discomfort. If you try a new supplement, consider how your body reacts.

- **Over-dependence:** Too heavily on supplements can lead to neglecting a balanced diet. Remember, they're meant to supplement your food intake, not replace it.
- **Quality control:** The supplement industry isn't as strictly regulated as food and medicine, meaning some products might not contain what they claim. Always choose reputable brands and check for third-party testing to ensure safety and effectiveness.

Before adding any new supplement to your regimen, it's crucial to consult with a healthcare provider or a registered dietitian. They can help you determine what's best for your individual needs.

Making Informed Choices: Guidelines for Safe Supplement Use

If you do decide to explore supplements, here are some guidelines to follow:

1. **Research reputable sources:** Choose brands with a good reputation and transparency about their ingredients and sourcing.
2. **Read labels carefully:** Consider ingredient lists and serving sizes. Be aware of added sugars, fillers, or artificial ingredients that might not serve your health goals.
3. **Educate yourself:** Understanding what's in your supplements and why you're taking them can help you make safer choices. Don't hesitate to ask questions if you're unsure about a product.

Key Takeaway

Navigating the world of sports supplements can be tricky, but by focusing on a balanced diet first and using supplements wisely, you can enhance your performance without compromising your health. Always prioritize real food, consult with healthcare professionals when needed, and choose supplements backed by research and quality assurance. Remember, being the best soccer player starts with understanding your body and fueling it properly!

CHAPTER 8:
OFF-SEASON TRAINING

The off-season is like a blank canvas for athletes—when the pressure's off, but the opportunity to grow is at its peak. This is when champions are made. It's easy to see the off-season as downtime, but it's where the real work begins. This is your chance to build a foundation that will carry you through the competitive grind of the season ahead.

Think about it: while others kick back, you're out there sharpening your skills, building strength, and mentally preparing to crush the competition. It's a chance to focus on what you need—whether that's improving your footwork, increasing your stamina, or developing that killer mindset that's going to keep you calm and collected in high-pressure moments.

The magic of the off-season is that it's fully in your control. There are no matches, no external pressure—just you, your goals, and your drive. Whether fine-tuning specific skills or putting together a cross-training plan to stay fresh, this is the time to do it.

OFF-SEASON TRAINING ROUTINES

Off-season is where the magic happens. When everyone else is chilling, this is your time to work, building the skills that'll make you unstoppable when the season starts. Here's how you turn the off-season into your secret weapon.

Creating a Balanced Training Schedule

Your off-season plan must hit all the right notes: skill drills, strength work, and game simulations. Think of it like a playlist—you wouldn't just play the same song on repeat, right? Mix it up!

- **Skill drills:** Daily footwork, passing accuracy, or shooting practice. It's all about repetition here—think Beckham bending a free kick 1,000 times before perfecting it.
- **Strength training:** Don't forget your body. Building strength (especially core and leg muscles) will help you hold your ground in matches.
- **Game simulations:** Scrimmage with friends, even if it's 3v3, to keep that game feel alive. You'll be sharper and more prepared for real competition.

Balancing your routine keeps things fresh and prevents burnout while ensuring you hit all aspects of development. Overload on one area, and you risk losing out elsewhere—consistency and variety are your keys to leveling up.

Incorporating Individual Skill Drills

Have you got a weak spot? This is the time to work on it. Off-season is perfect for focusing on individual weaknesses, whether your left foot, heading accuracy, or positioning.

- **Target-specific skills:** Work on ball control, dribbling, or long passes, one at a time. Focus on drills that challenge your weakness—like juggling with your weaker foot or setting up cones to perfect dribbling patterns.
- **Build muscle memory:** Continuous practice locks those skills into muscle memory. It's like learning to ride a bike—at first, it's wobbly, but soon it becomes second nature.

These are the details that team practices sometimes gloss over, so seize the chance to get laser-focused.

Simulating Game Scenarios

Training is only half the battle. You need to feel the heat of a real game, even when it's off-season. Small-sided games (like 3v3 or 5v5) are perfect for this.

- **Match-like intensity:** This helps you make quick decisions under pressure. The faster pace and limited space train you to think on your feet—something you'll thank yourself for later.
- **Adaptability:** Learning to read the game and adjust your play on the fly makes you a more versatile player. It's all about keeping your game IQ high.

You'll go back to regular matches more confident and mentally prepared, having sharpened your decision-making skills.

Monitoring Progress and Adaptations

Track everything! A training journal is like a roadmap for your progress.

- **Track your gains:** Writing down your goals, workouts, and improvements allows you to reflect on how far you've come. Did your pass accuracy improve? Is your stamina holding up better in scrimmages?
- **Adapt and adjust:** Keep tweaking your plan based on what's working (or isn't). The beauty of the off-season is the flexibility to try new things without the pressure of upcoming games.

Tracking progress gives you a clear picture of what's improving and needs more attention.

Key Takeaways

Off-season training isn't about grinding endlessly. It's about being smart with your time—balancing drills, strength work, and game simulations to cover all aspects of your game. Track your progress, stay adaptable, and when the season rolls around, you'll be miles ahead.

Importance of Rest and Recovery

Rest isn't just about kicking back and doing nothing—it's a secret weapon to becoming a better player. In the off-season, balancing hard work with proper recovery keeps you in the game, injury-free, and always improving.

Understanding the Body's Need for Rest

Your muscles need time to repair after all the intense training you're doing. When you take rest days, you're allowing them to recover and get stronger.

- **Muscle repair:** After training, your muscles need time to rebuild. Without rest, you're risking injury and long-term setbacks.
- **Prevent overtraining:** Ignoring your body's signals—like fatigue and soreness—can lead to burnout. Recognizing when you need a break is just as important as knowing when to push harder.

Recovery isn't about being lazy; it's about being smart and giving your body what it needs to perform at its best.

Incorporating Active Recovery

Rest doesn't always mean total inactivity. Sometimes, active recovery is the best way to bounce back while staying engaged.

- **Low-impact movement:** Activities like swimming, yoga, or easy cycling keep blood flowing to your muscles, which helps reduce soreness without putting too much strain on your body.
- **Stay engaged:** Mixing up recovery activities keeps things fun and prevents you from getting bored. Plus, active recovery helps improve flexibility and mobility—two key factors for any soccer player.

Active recovery helps you feel fresh while working on your overall athleticism, keeping you in the groove without overdoing it.

Utilizing Sleep for Recovery

Getting enough sleep is like refueling your body and mind. Without quality sleep, all your hard work can go to waste.

- **Physical restoration:** During sleep, your body repairs tissues, builds muscle, and replenishes energy stores. Less sleep = slower recovery.
- **Mental clarity:** A good night's sleep also sharpens your focus, which means better decision-making and quicker reactions on the field.

Create a sleep-friendly environment: cool room, no screens before bed, and a consistent sleep schedule. It'll make a huge difference in how rested and ready you feel.

Integrating Mental Recovery Techniques

Soccer isn't just physical—keeping your mind in the game is just as important.

- **Mental reset:** Practices like meditation, mindfulness, or journaling help you stay calm, focused, and ready to go. Soccer can be stressful, and mental recovery gives your mind the rest it needs to recharge.
- **Reduce stress:** By practicing mindfulness or even taking time to visualize success on the field, you're giving yourself a mental edge. A clear head leads to better focus and decision-making during games.

Mental wellness helps keep your passion alive and ensures that you're returning mentally refreshed and physically rested.

Rest and recovery aren't optional—they're the backbone of sustainable progress. By caring for your body and mind, you'll avoid injuries, stay fresh, and come back stronger. That's how you keep your performance at its peak.

Cross-Training Benefits

When you think of becoming a better soccer player, the answer might not just be more soccer. Cross-training—mixing in other sports—can seriously level up your game. It's not only fun, but it'll also make you stronger, smarter, and less prone to burnout.

Improving Overall Fitness

Different sports challenge muscles and give your body a more well-rounded fitness boost.

- **Balanced fitness:** Basketball can build agility, swimming strengthens your core and endurance, and tennis sharpens your reflexes. This variety helps you avoid hitting a plateau in your fitness.
- **Injury prevention:** By working on muscles you don't always use in soccer, you're building up resilience. A stronger overall fitness profile means fewer chances of getting sidelined with injuries.

Incorporating diverse sports keeps your body guessing, which leads to new strengths that carry over to the soccer field.

Learning Transferable Skills

You'd be surprised how much other sports can boost your soccer game.

- **Agility and coordination:** Think about how basketball improves footwork and quick changes in direction or how baseball hones hand-eye coordination. These skills translate directly into soccer performance—whether it's making faster decisions or improving your reaction time.

- **Game IQ:** Playing sports with different strategies, like learning to read plays in football or hockey, helps you approach soccer with fresh ideas. You'll gain a tactical edge by understanding how to adapt to different scenarios on the field.

The more sports you experience, the more dynamic and adaptable you become as a player.

Reducing the Risk of Burnout

Let's face it—too much of the same thing can get dull, even when you love it. Cross-training is the perfect way to keep things exciting.

- **Stay motivated:** Switching to a new sport during the off-season keeps you mentally engaged. You're still active, but it feels like a break from the usual grind.
- **Reignite passion:** Trying new activities can make you appreciate soccer even more when you return. Discovering other sports you enjoy helps you find balance and stay motivated long-term.

Keeping your training routine varied will help you avoid mental fatigue and keep your love for soccer alive.

Fostering Social Connections and Teamwork

Cross-training also allows you to meet new people and develop teamwork in different settings.

- **New teammates, new lessons:** Playing sports outside of soccer helps you build friendships and learn to communicate with various teammates. You'll learn how to work with different types of players, which boosts your ability to gel with teammates back on the soccer field.

- **Adapting to different teams:** Experiencing different team dynamics teaches you to adapt quickly—something that'll help you when playing in new formations or with new teammates in soccer.

The more varied your experiences, the better you'll get at working as a team.

Key Takeaways

Cross-training is a game-changer. It strengthens your body, sharpens your mind, and helps you avoid burning out. By exploring other sports, you're laying the foundation for better soccer performance and renewing your love for the game.

Setting Personal Goals for Off-Season Training

Setting personal goals during the off-season is key to becoming your best soccer player. It's not just about training harder but training smarter. Here's how to set goals that will keep you focused and motivated, all while making real progress on the field.

Creating SMART Goals

Start by setting **SMART goals**. These are the goals that are:

- **Specific:** What exactly do you want to achieve? Whether it's improving your dribbling or building endurance, be clear about it.

- **Measurable:** Track your progress. Can you run a mile in under 6 minutes? How many goals can you score in practice?
- **Achievable:** Don't aim for the impossible. Set goals that challenge you but are within reach.
- **Relevant:** Make sure your goals align with your overall soccer ambitions. If you're a forward, maybe work on finishing; if you're a defender, sharpen your tackling.
- **Time-bound:** Give yourself a deadline. For example, aim to master a new skill by the end of the off-season.

By following this framework, your goals will be more structured and meaningful, giving you the direction you need.

Reflection on Past Performance

Take some time to analyze your performance from last season. Ask yourself:

- Where did I struggle most? Maybe it was stamina or ball control.
- What feedback did my coach give me? This insight can be gold when setting your goals.
- What am I good at? Knowing your strengths can help you set ambitious but realistic goals, pushing you further.

This reflection process helps in crafting goals that target specific areas for improvement while building on your existing strengths.

Breaking Larger Goals Into Milestones

Big goals can feel overwhelming, but breaking them down into smaller steps makes them much more manageable. For example, if your goal is to improve your endurance, start by setting weekly running targets. Achieving these small wins keeps you motivated and on track.

Don't forget to regularly assess your progress and adjust your plan if needed. If you're ahead of schedule, push yourself a little more. If you're struggling, tweak the steps. Celebrate those small victories—they add up to major improvements!

Accountability and Support Systems

Sharing your goals with others, like teammates or coaches, can help keep you accountable. When someone else knows what you're working towards, you will likely stick with it. Plus, getting feedback along the way from your support system keeps you motivated and offers helpful insights you might not see yourself.

Working with teammates on goal setting also builds a sense of shared mission. Whether it's improving a team strategy or individual skills, collaboration fosters a strong sense of camaraderie.

Key Takeaways

By setting clear, structured goals, you can make the most of your off-season and ensure long-term development. Your goals become the roadmap to achieving your soccer dreams, and sticking to them will give you that edge when the next season kicks off.

CHAPTER 9:
BUILDING TEAM CHEMISTRY

Trust and respect might not show up on the stat sheet, but they're the real MVPs of any soccer team. Without them, even the most talented group of players can fall apart. Soccer isn't just about individual skills like dribbling or shooting—it's about teamwork. And a team only works well when every player trusts and respects one another.

Think about it: you must trust that your teammate will be in the right spot when you pass the ball or make that crucial run. And you have to respect each player's role on the field, from the goalkeeper to the striker. It's the glue that holds everything together. When you've got trust and respect, you're not just a bunch of players—you're a unit, a team that can take on anything.

Trust is built through communication and shared experiences, while respect comes from appreciating everyone's unique strengths. If you're missing either one, things start to fall apart—players clash, mistakes multiply, and suddenly, you're not playing as a team anymore. Let's explain why trust and respect are key to turning a group of athletes into a winning squad.

IMPORTANCE OF TRUST AND RESPECT

Why it matters: Soccer isn't just about how fast you can dribble or how hard you can shoot—it's about working together as a team. And to do that, you've got to trust and respect your teammates. Without these, even the best players can feel like they're playing alone. Let's dive into why trust and respect are the secret sauce for a winning team.

Building Trust Through Communication

- Talking things out, whether it's about tactics or how you're feeling before a big game, **helps everyone get on the same page**. The more you talk, the better you understand each other, and that's where trust starts.
- **Clear communication** makes everything smoother—less drama and fewer mix-ups. A quick chat can clear the air before things get tense.
- When players feel comfortable **sharing their thoughts**, it's like building a team where everyone has each other's backs. No one's left out; you know you can count on each other during the game.
- **On the field**, trust shows up when you pass the ball, knowing your teammate is ready, or when they cover for you if you mess up. You trust them because you've built that connection through talking.

Respecting Each Player's Role

- Whether you're scoring goals, blocking shots, or running up and down the field, **every player's role is important**. You can't win with just one star—everyone has a job.

- Showing **respect for what your teammates do** keeps the team fired up. Cheer on the defender who makes a big tackle or the midfielder who controls the game. It's not just about scoring.

- **Respecting everyone's contribution** makes the whole team feel included. When each player knows they're valued, they push harder for the team.

- Celebrating the different **strengths** your teammates bring boosts morale and helps everyone feel good about what they bring to the team.

Handling Conflicts With Respect

- Let's face it: arguments happen, whether it's over who should've taken the shot or why someone missed a pass; **how you handle conflict** matters.

- **Be respectful when there's a disagreement:** Don't blow up or ignore the problem. Instead, listen to the other person's saying and figure out how to move forward.

- **Respectful conflict resolution:** keeps things from spiraling into drama so the team can stay focused on playing, not fighting.

- When teammates resolve issues with respect, **trust** strengthens because everyone knows that even in tough times, they've got each other's respect.

Creating a Safe Space for Vulnerability

- A great team is one where players feel comfortable enough to be real with each other. Whether it's admitting you had a bad game or sharing something personal, **you've got to have each other's backs**.
- When teammates feel safe to open up, it **builds stronger bonds**. Suddenly, it's not just about soccer— you've got a deeper connection with your teammates.
- **Being open with each other** makes the team more supportive. You don't have to pretend to be perfect, and that creates an atmosphere where everyone grows.
- **On the field,** trust grows because you understand where your teammates are coming from. It's like knowing they've got your back, not just in the game but in life.

Key Takeaways:

- Trust and respect are what hold a team together. They make everything smoother—whether you're talking tactics, fixing a problem, or playing together.
- Building a team where everyone feels valued means you'll play better and have more fun.
- As a player, focusing on trust and respect will help you become a better teammate, and when that happens, the whole team wins.

Trust and respect don't just show up—you've got to work on them. But when you do, the game changes for the better!

TEAM-BUILDING ACTIVITIES AND EXERCISES

The goal of the Subpoint

This section is all about bringing your team closer, strengthening bonds, and building a strong sense of unity that translates into better teamwork and smoother play on the field.

Set of Supporting Ideas

Icebreaker Games

When you're part of a team, getting comfortable with each other is half the battle. Icebreaker games are perfect for breaking down those initial walls. They help players loosen up, reduce social barriers, and make teammates feel more connected. Whether "Two Truths and a Lie" or a silly relay race, these games spark conversations and form the foundation for stronger relationships.

Trust-Fall Exercises

You may have heard of trust falls—yeah, they're a little nerve-wracking, but that's the point! It's all about building trust. In a game like soccer, knowing that your teammate has your back can be a game-changer. These exercises push players to be vulnerable and rely on one another. Plus, when done right, they seriously boost team morale and strengthen the squad's overall cohesion.

Group Challenges

Want to bring out the best in your team? Throw in some group challenges. These competitive games force everyone to collaborate, strategize, and solve problems together. When you achieve something as a group, it reinforces how crucial teamwork is for success. A little healthy competition amps up the synergy, and by the end of these challenges, you'll see how much more cohesive the team becomes.

Community Service Projects

Sometimes, stepping off the soccer field can bring a team closer than ever. Doing community service together—whether it's cleaning up a park or organizing a local charity drive—creates meaningful, shared experiences that foster empathy. Bonding outside soccer strengthens relationships, and that positive energy carries right back onto the field.

Key Takeaways

Engaging in these team-building activities brings your team closer and boosts individual confidence, trust, and communication. A united team is a stronger team, and when you feel like you truly belong, your on-field performance and satisfaction skyrocket.

ENCOURAGING OPEN COMMUNICATION

Goal of the Subpoint

Open and honest communication can transform a group of players into a well-oiled machine. This section will show you how fostering open dialogue leads to better teamwork, smoother problem-solving, and overall stronger team performance.

Set of Supporting Ideas

Establishing Open Channels of Communication
Creating a space where everyone feels comfortable sharing their thoughts is crucial. Whether suggesting a new play or expressing frustration, players who communicate openly are more likely to solve problems before they blow up. Encouraging interaction on and off the field makes players feel heard, valued, and part of the team.

Regular Team Meetings
Scheduling team check-ins isn't just for the pros. Regular team meetings allow everyone to talk through challenges, set goals, and celebrate wins. By making feedback part of the routine, you create a culture of constant growth and improvement. These meetings also give players a voice, empowering them to suggest changes or share ideas that could take the team to the next level.

Utilizing Technology for Communication
There's no reason communication should stop when practice ends. Using group chats or apps like WhatsApp or Slack keeps the conversation going. Whether organizing practice times or sharing tactics, these platforms help the whole team stay on the same page. Plus, it's a great way to stay engaged with each other, even when you're off the pitch.

Constructive Feedback Practices

Learning how to give and receive feedback is key to growth as a team. Teach your teammates how to focus on the positive while addressing areas for improvement. Encouraging constructive feedback builds trust and camaraderie, making it easier to support each other through tough games or training sessions, reinforcing the good stuff. That's how you keep your motivation high.

Key Takeaways

Open communication is the secret weapon to building trust and boosting teamwork. By creating an environment where players can freely share, offer feedback, and stay connected, you'll not only improve team dynamics but also strengthen bonds off the field.

ROLE OF LEADERSHIP WITHIN THE TEAM

Leadership is more than just wearing the captain's armband. It's about taking responsibility, setting the tone, and bringing the best out of your teammates. Let's dive into what makes leadership such a game-changer on and off the pitch.

1. **Defining leadership roles**

    Leadership isn't just the job of your captain. Every team benefits when multiple players step up, guiding the group toward success. Players like **Virgil van Dijk** of Liverpool show how strong leadership isn't just about yelling commands—it's about being a pillar of confidence. Van Dijk commands the defense but also inspires those around him to up their game. When leadership roles are clearly defined—whether you're the team captain or a seasoned player leading by example, everyone knows what's expected of them.

Being a leader means guiding younger or less experienced players. Think of how **Lionel Messi** mentored young talent at Barcelona, helping players like Ansu Fati grow into their roles. A leader on the team should be willing to share knowledge, help others improve, and provide stability when things get tough on the field.

2. **Empowering players to take the initiative**

    Leadership doesn't have to be reserved for just one or two players. Every player should feel empowered to lead in their own way. Encouraging everyone to step up creates a culture of accountability and boosts teamwork. Players like **Kevin De Bruyne** show leadership in how they control the game and inspire others to step into key roles when necessary.

At practice, let everyone take turns leading drills or running team huddles. When players take ownership of their training, they stay more engaged and motivated. This kind of initiative makes a huge difference on game day when players can take charge during crucial moments, even without waiting for instructions from the coach.

3. **Modeling sportsmanship and attitude**

    A great leader models sportsmanship and sets the attitude for the team. When **Megan Rapinoe** steps on the field, she isn't just focused on winning; she's focused on playing with integrity. Leaders show the rest of the team how to handle victory with humility and how to face losses with grace. This attitude is contagious, and soon, the whole team adopts the same mindset.

When players see their leaders treating teammates, referees, and opponents with respect, they're likely to follow. Fostering this positive environment translates to a more cohesive and resilient team, one that supports each other no matter what.

4. **Recognizing leaders beyond captains**

   While captains are often the most visible leaders, every player has the potential to lead in their own way. Players like **N'Golo Kanté** don't need an armband to lead—they lead through actions. Kanté's relentless work ethic and humble nature have made him a role model in every team he's played for. Recognizing leadership qualities in players who may not speak the loudest but show consistency, reliability, and skill can boost team morale.

By encouraging diverse forms of leadership, you create a team that thrives on creativity and cooperation. Everyone brings something unique to the table, and tapping into those strengths makes for a stronger, more unified team.

Key Takeaways

Leadership is the backbone of any great soccer team. It's not just about having one player call the shots; it's about everyone stepping up, taking responsibility, and pushing the team forward. By fostering leadership in all players, modeling sportsmanship, and recognizing leaders beyond the captain, you create a team environment where everyone feels empowered, respected, and ready to give their best.

CHAPTER 10:
GAME DAY PREPARATION

Pre-match rituals and routines are like the secret sauce to game-day success. They're not just quirky habits or superstitions; they help you get in the zone, calm your nerves, and mentally prepare to give your best performance. Whether you're lacing up your boots a certain way or leading a team huddle, these rituals can make the difference between feeling scattered and being laser-focused when the whistle blows. Let's dive into why these routines are so important and how they can help you dominate on the field.

PRE-MATCH RITUALS AND ROUTINES

Imagine this: the sun is shining, the crowd is buzzing, and it's game day! The excitement is palpable, but how do you channel that energy into an amazing performance? That's where pre-match rituals and routines come in! They help you prepare both mentally and physically, giving you the edge you need to dominate the field.

1. **Importance of consistency**

   Establishing a consistent pre-match routine can be a game-changer. Think of it like the secret sauce that helps you manage those pre-game jitters. **Cristiano Ronaldo** is known for his meticulous approach to preparation. His routines help him focus and signal that it's time to perform. When you have a routine, your body recognizes the cues that say, "Hey, we're ready to go!"

   A well-prepared mindset can significantly improve your performance. Feeling confident and familiar with your routine reduces anxiety and enhances focus, so you can concentrate on the match ahead rather than stressing about it.

2. **Personalization of rituals**

   Everyone is different, which makes finding your perfect routine so important. What calms one player may energize another. **Alex Morgan** has the unique pre-match rituals that get her in the right headspace before a game. Maybe you find that stretching, listening to your favorite pump-up song, or practicing mental visualization works best for you.

   Experiment with various activities—perhaps try deep breathing, light jogging, or journaling your goals for the match. Tailoring your routine to your psychological preferences can significantly affect your performance.

3. **The role of teammates**

   Pre-match rituals aren't just about individual preparation and building team spirit. Engaging in collective rituals can strengthen group cohesion and foster a sense of unity. Think about teams like **Barcelona**; they often partake in group huddles or chants that bring them together and build trust.

These bonding activities create lasting memories and enhance the atmosphere on game day. When you're connected with your teammates, you're more likely to perform well together. Plus, you'll look back on those shared experiences with a smile!

4. **Timing of routines**

   Timing is everything! Arriving early on game day allows you to engage in your pre-match rituals without feeling rushed. You don't want to be that player scrambling to get ready while the kickoff is looming. Having enough time ensures you can pace your activities, preventing anxiety and allowing you to focus fully on your performance.

Adequate warm-up time is essential, too. It prepares your body physically so you're ready to hit the ground running as soon as the whistle blows. Consider a combination of dynamic stretches and light exercises to get your muscles warmed up and your heart rate elevated.

Key Takeaways

Pre-match rituals and routines are vital for enhancing focus, building team cohesion, and improving performance on game day. By developing consistent practices that suit your unique needs and engaging with your teammates in shared rituals, you set yourself up for success. Remember, the right mindset can make all the difference—so find what works for you and get ready to shine on the pitch!

Pre-Match Rituals and Routines: The Power of Warm-Up Exercises and Stretches

Picture this: You step onto the field, the crowd's buzz fills the air, and your heart races. But before you dive into the game, there's one critical step: the warm-up. Think of warm-ups as your secret sauce to becoming a top player, just like legends like Lionel Messi and Cristiano Ronaldo prep before a match. Here's why those few minutes matter more than you might think!

Physical Readiness

A solid warm-up routine isn't just about looking cool; it's about getting your body ready for action. When you gradually increase your heart rate and circulation, you're:

- **Preventing injuries:** Starting slowly helps your muscles and joints get ready for the intense movements ahead. No one wants to be sidelined because of a preventable injury, right?

- **Boosting performance:** Engaging in dynamic stretches—like leg swings and high knees—improves your flexibility and range of motion. This means you can execute those flashy moves without a hitch!

- **Targeting soccer-specific muscles:** Warm-ups should focus on the muscles you'll use during the game. Think of lunges, squats, and light jogging—these get your legs, hips, and core primed for all those quick bursts of energy you'll need.

Mental Focus

Warm-ups aren't just for your body; they're also a time to sharpen your mind. As you stretch and move, use this time to:

- **Visualize your game plan:** Picture yourself executing strategies and making plays. Whether nailing that through a ball or setting up a perfect cross, visualization helps you prepare mentally for the challenges ahead.

- **Engage as a team:** Warm-up time is a perfect opportunity to build that team chemistry. When you laugh, chat, and bond during warm-ups, you create a collective energy that can elevate everyone's performance.

- **Clear your mind:** Concentrating on your warm-up movements can help wash away distracting thoughts and nerves. Focus on each stretch and each drill, and you'll feel more centered as kickoff approaches.

The Significance of Cool-Downs

Don't just rush off the field after the final whistle! Post-game stretches are just as important:

- **Aid recovery:** Stretching after a match reduces potential soreness and stiffness. It's like giving your body a thank-you note for all the hard work it just did!

- **Mental deflection:** Use cooldown time to think about your performance. What went well? What could be improved? This reflection can help you grow as a player.

- **Nurture team camaraderie:** Engaging in team cooldown activities—like light jogging and stretching—

fosters a sense of togetherness after a game, strengthening those bonds.

Incorporating Fun

Warm-ups don't have to be boring! Spice things up with some fun activities:

- **Games during warm-ups:** Incorporating fun drills or small-sided games can elevate the mood and create positive energy. Try mini-soccer matches or relay races to get everyone pumped up!
- **Challenging drills:** Think of warm-up drills that enhance teamwork and collaboration, like passing drills that require communication. This builds not just skills but also a sense of unity among teammates.

Key Takeaways

Warm-up and cool-down routines are essential for both physical and mental preparation. By mastering these techniques, you'll not only be physically ready for game day but also mentally sharp, reducing pre-game anxiety and setting the stage for optimal performance. So, before you step onto that pitch, remember to warm up, focus, and get ready to shine!

Pre-Match Rituals and Routines: Scouting the Opponent

The goal of the subpoint:

To highlight the strategic advantage of understanding and analyzing the opponent before match day, enabling players to approach the game confidently and quickly.

Research and Observation

Knowledge is power, especially in soccer. By gathering information about your opponent's strengths and weaknesses, you can tailor your game plan to exploit their vulnerabilities. Start by watching their previous matches—streaming services often have game footage. Look for patterns in how they play, whether they tend to push forward aggressively or how they react under pressure.

Key strategies to analyze

- **Formation tendencies:** Do they play with a back four or three? Understanding this helps you anticipate their defensive structure.
- **Key players:** Identify who makes their team tick. Is there a creative midfielder who pulls the strings? Knowing this allows you to mark them tightly or disrupt their flow.
- **Position-specific strategies:** Understand how different positions operate. For example, if their right back often overlaps with wings, you can strategize to exploit that space.

Team Collaboration

Scouting isn't a solo mission—it's a team effort! Discussing your findings with teammates can lead to better strategies. Have team meetings where everyone shares their observations. Maybe someone noticed that the opponent struggles with high pressing or lacks pace in their back line. Use this collective intelligence to craft a game plan that maximizes your team's strengths against their weaknesses.

Create Game-Specific Strategies

- Plan how to counter their strengths. If they have a powerful striker, consider how your defenders can double-team them or funnel them into less dangerous areas.
- Foster open communication during practice, allowing players to share insights and adapt based on your scouting report.

Adjusting Mindset

Going into a game, your mindset can be just as crucial as your physical preparation. Develop a flexible mentality that allows you to adjust based on the opponent's style. If you know they tend to be aggressive, prepare to keep your cool and not get rattled. Conversely, if they're more defensive, practice breaking down those formations.

Recognizing Psychological Aspects

- Understand how an opponent's reputation can affect their gameplay. If they're known for being physical, players might overcommit or become too cautious. Stay focused on your own game and how you can impose your style.

Practice Scenarios

Preparation doesn't stop at analysis; it should extend to your practice sessions. Create drills that mimic what you've learned about the opponent. If they like to play out from the back, set up situations where your team practices pressing effectively. Simulation game scenarios prepare you to face specific challenges head-on.

Role-Playing Strategies

- Use scrimmages to experiment with different formations or styles based on your scouting. This flexibility in practice will prepare you for whatever the game throws at you.

Key Takeaways

Understanding your opponent is like having a secret weapon. By investing time in scouting, collaborating with your teammates, adjusting your mindset, and preparing through practice, you'll create actionable strategies that boost your team's performance on match day. Remember, the best players are not just skilled but strategic thinkers who embrace preparation.

Structured Reflection

First off, let's talk about the importance of structured reflection. Looking back at your performance is like having a personal coach in your head. By reviewing your game, you highlight your strengths—those sweet moments when everything clicked—and pinpoint areas for improvement. Here's why it matters:

- **Identifying strengths:** When you recognize what you did well, it reinforces your confidence. Remember that sick assist you made? That's a highlight you can build on for the next game.

- **Constructive criticism:** You're not perfect (and that's okay!). Discussing where you can improve helps you grow. It's about taking feedback and using it as fuel for your development.

Team Feedback

Next, let's move to the collective side of things. Team feedback sessions are like a team huddle after a game—everyone's got a voice. This is crucial because:

- **Ownership and accountability:** When everyone shares their observations, it builds a sense of ownership. Everyone feels invested in the team's success and learns to hold each other accountable.
- **Strengthening bonds:** Analyzing the match together creates shared experiences. It's one thing to play together; it's another to learn together.

Mental Reinforcement

Now, don't forget the mental side! Reflecting on your mental strategies during the game is as important as looking at your physical performance. Here's how it can help:

- **Self-awareness:** By thinking about how you handled pressure or made decisions, you develop self-awareness. Did you freeze during a penalty? Time to strategize for next time!

- **Embracing challenges:** Adopting a growth mindset means seeing challenges as learning opportunities rather than setbacks. Every mistake is just another step toward improvement.

Setting Future Goals

Finally, let's look ahead. After your analysis, it's time to set some actionable goals for the future. This is where the magic happens:

- **Specific and measurable goals:** Setting clear targets helps you track progress. Want to improve your passing accuracy? Make it a goal to hit 80% in your next game.
- **Aligning objectives:** These discussions not only focus on personal growth but also help align with team goals. If everyone is on the same page, you'll see collective improvement.

CONCLUSION

As we wrap up our journey through "The Youth Soccer Handbook," it's time to reflect on the vital lessons we've covered and how they can shape you into a better soccer player. We've traveled from understanding basic techniques to mastering complex strategies, all while emphasizing the importance of mental toughness and teamwork. Let's revisit these important concepts one more time.

Firstly, mastering the fundamentals is crucial. Whether it's passing, dribbling, or shooting, these skills are the building blocks of your game. By honing these abilities, you sett yourself up for success on the pitch. However remember that learning doesn't stop at merely acquiring these skills; it involves continually refining and perfecting them through regular practice and drills. Consistency in practicing these fundamentals is what will truly make you stand out.

Next, we dove into advanced skill development, which builds on those fundamental techniques. These include sophisticated dribbling moves, precision shooting under pressure, and effective tackling and interception strategies. Mastering these advanced skills not only makes you a more versatile player but also instills a level of confidence that can turn the tide in high-stakes matches. The emphasis should be on integrating these advanced techniques seamlessly into your gameplay so that they become second nature during matches.

Understanding team strategies and formations was another key area we explored. Soccer is a team sport, and knowing how to function within various formations can give your team a tactical advantage. Whether it be the balanced 4-4-2 or the attacking 4-3-3, each formation has its own roles and responsibilities. Being adaptable and understanding your role within different formations ensures that you can contribute effectively to your team's success, regardless of the strategy.

We also highlighted the importance of mental preparedness. Developing concentration, overcoming performance anxiety, and setting realistic goals are essential for any athlete striving for excellence. These mental skills are just as critical as your physical abilities. Embracing a growth mindset allows you to view challenges as opportunities for improvement rather than obstacles. The mental toughness you develop will help you stay focused, maintain composure under pressure, and bounce back from setbacks.

Another significant aspect we discussed is fitness and conditioning. Endurance, strength, flexibility, and agility are all pillars of athletic performance. Proper conditioning means you'll have the stamina to perform consistently throughout a match and the resilience to avoid injuries. Incorporating varied training routines and focusing on both strength and mobility ensures you're well-rounded and prepared for the demands of the sport.

Nutrition played a pivotal role in our discussion as well. Fueling your body with the right nutrients before and after games can significantly enhance your performance and recovery. Understanding macronutrients, staying hydrated, and timing your meals properly contribute to your overall athletic prowess. Remember, what you put into your body directly affects how well you can perform and recover.

The off-season is not merely a break but an opportunity for continued growth. Structured training routines, rest, and cross-training can help you maintain and improve your skills when you're not in the main season. Setting personal goals during this time keeps you motivated and ready to return stronger.

Building team chemistry is something that cannot be overlooked. Trust, respect, and open communication create a cohesive environment where everyone can thrive. Engaging in team-building activities and fostering a supportive atmosphere ensures that every player feels valued and motivated. A united team, both on and off the field, can overcome challenges more effectively and celebrate successes together.

Finally, game day preparation involves more than just physical readiness. Establishing consistent pre-match rituals can reduce anxiety and enhance focus, while proper warm-up exercises prepare your body for the intensity of the game. Scouting opponents provides you with a strategic edge, and post-game analysis helps you learn and grow from each match.

Reflecting on your performance and setting future goals based on these reflections fosters a cycle of continuous improvement.

So, what does all of this mean for you? It means that your journey in soccer is just beginning, and there is always room to grow. Regular practice is crucial, as is being open to learning new techniques and strategies. Soccer is an ever-evolving sport, and staying up-to-date with the latest methods can keep you ahead.

Remember, teamwork and sportsmanship are the heart of soccer. How you interact with your teammates and opponents defines you as a player. Being a good teammate means supporting others, encouraging open communication, and demonstrating respect both on and off the field. It's about more than just winning; it's about playing the game with integrity and passion.

Adopting a growth mindset will be your biggest asset. Every game offers a new lesson, and every challenge is an opportunity to improve. Keep pushing your limits, stay resilient despite setbacks, and never stop striving for excellence. With dedication and the right attitude, you can achieve great things in soccer.

So, lace up your boots, confidently step onto the pitch, and embrace the exciting journey ahead. Your hard work, persistence, and love for the game will drive you forward. Remember, every champion was once a beginner who refused to give up. Stay committed, keep learning, and enjoy every moment of your soccer adventure.

REFERENCES

- Alliance Football Club. (2020). *Woman-in-red-and-white-soccer-jersey-shirt-and-black-shorts-running-on-field-during-daytime*. In Unsplash. https://unsplash.com/@alliancefc?utm_content=creditCopyText&utm_medium=referral&utm_source=unsplash

- Bonk, D., & Tamminen, K. A. (2021). *Athlete's perspectives of preparation strategies in open-skill sports*. Journal of Applied Sport Psychology, 1–21. https://doi.org/10.1080/10413200.2021.1875517

- Brampton Adult Soccer. (2023, May 20). *The benefits of youth soccer participation*. Brampton Adult Soccer; BAS. https://bramptonsoccer.com/the-benefits-of-youth-soccer-participation/

- Castle, J. (2017, October 25). *Eight gameday nutrition tips for young athletes*. Www.eatright.org. https://www.eatright.org/fitness/sports-and-athletic-performance/beginner-and-intermediate/8-gameday-nutrition-tips-for-young-athletes

- Cohn, P. (2019). *How a pregame routine helps athletes succeed | sports psychology articles.* Peaksports.com. https://www.peaksports.com/sports-psychology-blog/how-a-pregame-routine-helps-athletes-succeed/

- Cotter, R. (2019, June 10). *6-Week off-season training program for elite youth soccer: a high-low approach - simpliFaster.* SimpliFaster. https://simplifaster.com/articles/off-season-training-youth-soccer/

- Dodd, P., & Higginbotham, T. (2019). *The origins & evolution of soccer.* Study.com. https://study.com/academy/lesson/the-origins-evolution-of-soccer.html

- erica. (2019, August 16). *Off-season training for soccer: two coaches discuss what it takes - Erica Suter.* Erica Suter. https://ericasuter.com/off-season-training-for-soccer-two-coaches-discuss-what-it-takes/

- Gymlyx. (2024, September 9). *The ultimate soccer exercise plan: boost your agility, strength, and endurance in 2024 - gymlyx.com.* Gymlyx.com. https://gymlyx.com/soccer-exercise-plan/

- Hugh, P. (2024, February 21). *Exploring the significance of team chemistry in soccer.* Soccer Wizdom. https://soccerwizdom.com/2024/02/21/exploring-the-significance-of-team-chemistry-in-soccer/

- *Introduction to receiving and controlling.* (n.d.). Coaching American Soccer. https://coachingamericansoccer.com/introductions-to-soccer-skills/soccer-receiving-and-controlling/

- Izuddin Helmi Adnan. (2017). *Aerial photography of people playing soccer.* In Unsplash. https://unsplash.com/

photos/aerial-photography-of-people-playing-soccer-ndxwXAt0jpg

- Jobs in Football. (2024, January 1). *Soccer positions explained - complete guide (2023)*. Jobs in Football. https://jobsinfootball.com/blog/soccer-positions/

- Kruel, L. (2021, October 7). *Optimal scorer off-season preparation ⚽ 8-week full program*. TRUSTMYCOACH. https://trustmycoach.com/soccer-fitness/off-season-preparation/

- Leija, R. (2017). *Man playing soccer*. In Unsplash. https://unsplash.com/photos/man-playing-soccer-Qlrcw3yOKec

- *Lesson 5: Roles and responsibilities of each position*. (2020, January 5). SoccerDrive.com. https://www.soccerdrive.com/learn-how-to-coach-soccer/youth-soccer-positions

- *Lesson 7: Fundamental soccer skills*. (2020, January 8). SoccerDrive.com. https://www.soccerdrive.com/learn-how-to-coach-soccer/fundamental-skills

- Mazanec, R. (2023, May 19). *What are sports rituals and do they make you play better?* Www.ncsasports.org. https://www.ncsasports.org/blog/the-benefit-of-sport-rituals

- Msipa, N. (2020). *Man in blue shirt playing soccer during daytime*. In Unsplash. https://unsplash.com/photos/man-in-blue-shirt-playing-soccer-during-daytime-ALv-6qS5bis

- My Profit Tutor. (2022). *A group of people holding up their hands*. In Unsplash. https://unsplash.com/photos/a-group-of-people-holding-up-their-hands-0BmvPTh45gM

- Nationwide Children's. (2023). *Game day fueling plan for athletes.* Www.nationwidechildrens.org. https://www.nationwidechildrens.org/specialties/sports-medicine/sports-medicine-articles/game-day-fueling-plan-for-athletes

- Pauloneal. (2024a, June 17). *The history and evolution of soccer: a journey through time.* Cochrane Wolves Football Club. https://www.cochranewolvesfc.ca/the-history-and-evolution-of-soccer-a-journey-through-time/

- Pauloneal. (2024b, August 21). *The significance of teamwork in soccer: building success together.* Cochrane Wolves Football Club. https://www.cochranewolvesfc.ca/the-significance-of-teamwork-in-soccer-building-success-together/

- Porter, I. (2024, May 16). *The power of pre-match routines.* Forward Drive Psych. https://www.forwarddrivepsychology.com/post/the-power-of-pre-match-routines

- Preiato, D. (2021, December 3). *Cross-training: what it is and how to get started.* Healthline. https://www.healthline.com/health/fitness/cross-training

- Purcell, L. K. (2013). *Sport nutrition for young athletes.* Paediatrics & Child Health, *18*(4), 200–205. https://doi.org/10.1093/pch/18.4.200

- Salvo Soccer Club. (2024, May 13). *The benefits of teamwork in youth soccer & how to foster it.* Salvo Soccer. https://www.salvosoccer.org/news/the-benefits-of-teamwork-in-youth-soccer-how-to-foster-it

- Sentongo, T. (2023, February 28). *What young athletes should eat before and after the game - UChicago medicine.* Www. uchicagomedicine.org. https://www.uchicagomedicine. org/forefront/pediatrics-articles/2023/march/what-young-athletes-should-eat-before-and-after-the-game
- Snow, S. (n.d.). *A player-centered curriculum for US youth soccer clubs.* https://cdn2.sportngin.com/attachments/ document/0090/7006/US_Youth_Soccer_Player_ Development_Model.pdf
- *The art of soccer skills: training techniques for champions.* (2024). Playerdata.com. https://www.playerdata.com/blog/ soccer-skills-training-techniques-for-champions
- *The basic rules of soccer: a complete guide | soccer.com.* (2022). Soccer.com. https://www.soccer.com/guide/rules-of-soccer-guide
- Union, P. (2024). *Youth | the importance of off-season training | Philadelphia Union.* Philadelphia Union. https://www. philadelphiaunion.com/news/off-season-training
- *What are the rules? • the 17 laws of soccer explained.* (2021). Mt. Lebanon Soccer Association. https://mlsa.demosphere-secure.com/referee/laws-of-the-game
- YTP Sports. (2024). *Fitness training and drill guide for soccer players.* YTP Sports. https://ytpsports.com/blog/f/ fitness-training-and-drill-guide-for-soccer-players